ABOUT THE AUTHORS

Ed and Alan Shimp are probably best known for their award-winning "Profspop" channel on YouTube. The channel features the comedic father and son duo in educational videos including "The Adventures of Ed and Alan," "Good and Well Grammar," and "Cultural Moments with Ed and Alan." The pair were named among the top ten "EDU Gurus" by YouTube. Alan and Ed are obsessive film fans who spend hours watching film and debating the finer points of cinema.

Alan is a precocious 18-year-old law student at the UCLA School of Law pursuing a specialty in entertainment law. He graduated of Penn State University in 2017, with a BA in history and minors in film and media studies. He is the founder and president of the Happy Valley Film Club and loves classic cinema.

Ed has an MFA in directing from DePaul University, and a BFA in acting from Penn State University. He has worked as a writer, actor, director, producer and adjunct instructor. Additionally, as the homeschooling parent of a profoundly gifted child, Ed has blogged extensively about fatherhood, homeschooling and giftedness.

THE
FilmFan
Handbook

Volume Two
Filmmaking

Alan G. Shimp
Edward Shimp

For Ginger

CONTENTS

PREFACE

Experts say that the best place to view a movie is about 2/3 of the way back in the auditorium at a 60-degree angle to the screen, but slightly off-center to improve the surround sound effect. This may be the best place to immerse yourself in the world of the film, but to understand a film completely, consider the 10,000-foot view. Being immersed in the experience is great, but you can't really appreciate the full scope of film without getting some distance from it.

This effort in writing about film appreciation began by taking an informal survey of people we met. "Why do you watch movies?" we'd asked. Without exception, the first response was, "To be entertained." When we asked what it means to be entertained, the answers got a lot sketchier, and when we asked how they might get the most entertainment out of the movie-going experience, people were at a total loss. We explore those questions and much more in our four-volume handbook.

Did you enjoy the last movie you saw? Were you entertained? It's simple enough to recall whether you liked a movie or not but reflecting on why you liked or disliked a movie is more challenging. Most people don't stop to think about that, but the ability to be discerning improves your ability to be "entertained."

It turns out that the best way to maximize your movie-going experience is to have a greater appreciation for what it takes to create that experience. Really, it's no different from any other domain. Anyone can watch a baseball game or play a game of chess and enjoy themselves, but if you really want to get the most out of the experience, you need to gain a deeper understanding of the discipline.

However, we believe that film is more significant than those other domains. Communication is central to our existence. If you were to lose all your senses (sight, hearing, touch, etc.), you wouldn't be able to experience life; and if you couldn't comprehend and evaluate that sensory input, you would hardly be alive.

Watching a film is certainly an ersatz experience. Watching a film about Spain, for example, isn't the same as going to Spain. However, if you're unable to actually travel to Spain, you can at least get some appreciation for what that would be like. Indeed, not only can a film take you to places you haven't been, it can also take you to places that don't exist, or let you view things from a perspective you don't have. Further, the more fully you appreciate what your senses are taking in, the more fulfilling your experience will be.

Unfortunately, to cover everything there is to know about film would probably require a hundred or more volumes but turning readers into experts isn't the intention of these books. The objective is to take moviegoers beyond passive viewership, without getting bogged down in tedious technicalities.

Film appreciation is not about having an encyclopedic knowledge of film history, but about having the ability to evaluate a film based on its content and context. Accordingly, the first two volumes of our handbook will discuss "content" and the second two volumes will look at the "context."

Content is anything that exists entirely within the film itself. Any part of the film which can be observed in the frame is part of the content. It's plainly observable by the viewer and is forever unchanging because it is fixed in its medium. Two elements combine to create the content, "narrative" and "filmmaking":

- **Narrative** comprises the elements, structure, and mythology of a film's story.
- **Filmmaking** is about the practical process of creating a film, and it includes the art and technical skills that go into constructing a film.

Context, on the other hand, is the sum of the external factors that shape the movie-going experience. Context is the circumstances in which a film is both created and viewed. While the content is immutable, the context is ever shifting and will vary from one observer to the next. Context can be subdivided into "culture" and "control."

- **Culture** influences how and why a film is made, and it's important to note that a film may take on a new significance if it is viewed under a different cultural paradigm. Social, political, economic, technological, and educational circumstances (among others) will affect both the creation and reception of a film.
- **Control** is the "business" part of show business. There are many power brokers vying to influence the content of a film and how it is seen. This volume discusses how these influencers combine efforts to regulate what you see.

We freely admit that you can miss a lot of details from the 10,000-foot view, but our hope is that these volumes will be a first step toward a more thorough investigation and appreciation of film. It's completely intentional that we avoid obscure references, and infrequently invoke the use of detailed examples in these books. While examples are referenced, it should be plain from the context why they are important. A thorough knowledge of films is not necessary to appreciate these books; it hardly makes sense to bolster an argument with references to unfamiliar examples. While there is certainly a place for well-documented academic or reference books, citing copious examples can weigh down and confound an overview.

Preface

Writing these volumes was a joyful process, as each thing we wrote about seemed more exciting than the last. At every turn, we concluded that the current subject was worthy of its own book. Like the proverbial (perhaps clichéd) kids in the candy store, we were giddy about every new way we conceived of looking at film and often found ourselves doing more talking than writing.

We hope that you will be as giddy reading these books as we were in writing them. We're certain that each new section will have you thinking about film in a new way.

- Alan & Ed

CHAPTER ONE

FILMMAKING

In Barbra Streisand's Academy Award acceptance speech for *Funny Girl* (1968), she infamously said she'd like to "thank all the little people." The "little people," the lower-profile members of a film's production, are indispensable. Look at the credits for any movie, especially a recent one, and you will see a lengthy list of unknowns. *Iron Man 3* (2013), for example, credits 3,310 people as having worked on the production. Every "little person's" effort is reflected in the final product.

In this volume, we'll discuss film technology and techniques, as well as the contributions of filmmaking professionals such as producers, directors, screenwriters, production designers, actors, editors, and composers. However, no single book could fully explain the contributions of everyone working on a film. Further, for every person who receives a credit, there are many connected to the film who are left out. Think of the secretaries, interns, custodial staff, and more who don't receive credit.

Film is arguably the most collaborative art form in existence. Every film involves a unique mix of personalities who come together to create a completed product. If anything, the importance of producers and directors comes more from their ability to lead and motivate everyone else to create a coherent final product than from their own artistic ability, especially since filmmaking professionals of all statures, big and little, tend to have extreme personalities. In particular, "above-the-line" talent (a budget-related term which refers largely to creatives like actors and directors whose pay is flexible, while "below-the-line" professionals are more technical and logistical in their responsibilities and have fixed salaries) tend to have significant egos, theoretically justified by their experience. Perhaps this is because of the risks inherent in making a film.

After all, making a film is not like creating a product on an assembly line. Filmmakers come together to make one film once, and it exists as a single work of art. Yes, you can make copies of a motion picture, but a film exists conceptually more than it does physically. A roll of film or the digital equivalent is a piece of equipment used to play the ideas that the film's cast and crew have brought to life. In a typical industry, if one unit of a product doesn't pass quality control standards, that won't necessarily mean that the other thousand being made won't turn out just fine, and refinements can be made on future production. In film, there's one product, and the filmmakers have one chance to get it right.

Of course, one way that the film industry is similar to a typical industry is that while every film is different, most films are created through roughly the same process. This standardization is precisely because of the variability and risk of the production. If hundreds of people, many of whom have never met one another before, are going to work together and create something worthwhile, there must be standardized processes that everyone can rely on, so that they all have a sort of common language. There are predefined jobs that need to be filled, a set process that needs to be completed, and common terminology which allows the creative professionals to communicate their ideas and intentions to one another.

The most successful person working on a production is the one who doesn't keep other people waiting. At every stage, there's something holding up progress. Major productions are a multimillion-dollar game of hot potato. They cannot be cobbled together in an ad hoc fashion. Each professional must show up prepared, and not interfere with the work of others. This, naturally, makes a film production a massive exercise in project management. The time, budget, logistics, supply chain, and contracts all have to be negotiated and planned carefully to minimize the amount of time that people spend waiting for others. Time is money, and money is a very limited resource for filmmakers. Even a big-budget production presumably *needs* its budget, and therefore it offsets an abundance of resources with additional complications. Everything here adds up to make film unique both as an art form and as a business.

The making of a film passes through three phases: production, distribution, and exhibition. Distribution and exhibition are important for the industry, but the artistry and the creation of the film itself fall entirely within production.

Film production companies can either be independent or are owned and operated by distributors. Some of their names may be only vaguely familiar. For example, American Zoetrope was created by George Lucas and Francis Ford Coppola in 1969. They have produced more than 75 films including *The Godfather* (1972) and *American Graffiti* (1973), and they have won 15 academy awards, and yet most people would not be able to recall their name. Other production companies are owned by large corporations who also distribute films. For example, Marvel Studios, the production company that makes most of the films based on Marvel Comics, is now a subsidiary of the Disney Corporation. It is easy to confuse production

companies with the distributors that own them. For example, Disney (the corporation and distributor) also owns Disney Animation and Disney Live Action (production companies). Paramount (the corporation and distributor) produces films under the Paramount name as well as Paramount Animation and Paramount Players (production companies).

The production process involves four stages: development, pre-production, production, and post-production. Development involves the decision to make a film and gathering the talent, script, and finances to do so. Development is often a balancing act where investors may not want to invest without certain talent attached to the project, and talent may not want to join without assurance that the project is funded. Both talent and money might want to see changes to the script before committing, assuming there is a script. That's not always the case. Talent and money are often committed to doing sequels or adaptations before the script is written.

After development, the film enters pre-production. Pre-production is the planning phase. Scripts are edited, storyboards drawn, locations scouted, and scenes rehearsed. Poorly executed pre-production planning can doom a film before the cameras ever roll. On the other hand, some believe that planning is the enemy of creativity, and even the most airtight plan will encounter unexpected complications. The amount of creative spontaneity in a film is often the result of a battle between the producers and the above-the-line talent. It's all about the money.

The film then passes into the main stage of the production, in which the actual shooting of the film takes place. This is the culmination of all the deal-making and planning that took place previously and is where the above-the-line talent like actors and directors have their greatest degree of control.

The post-production usually runs concurrently with the production phase. The main concern of post-production is editing, and it's best to begin a rough cut as soon as possible. The creation of visual effects, the film's scoring, and any modifications to the sound are also part of post-production, but it's up to the editor to put these elements together. At this point, the film cycles through several rounds of editing before finally becoming a finished product. So, while the post-production stage begins with the production stage, it continues well after the production stage ends.

From this point, the film moves on to the distribution phase, which will be examined more closely in Volume 3 of this series. Remarkably, many independent films will complete post-production without any plans for distribution. The producers are gambling that once the film is made, it can attract the interest of a distributor at a film festival. Film distribution is not entirely unlike distributing other products. It's all about getting it into the hands (or in this case before the eyes) of the customer.

Every production is unique, but each requires the efforts of producers and above-the-line talent, as well as all those "little people." With luck, what can be a fickle, frustrating, and financially frightening process will somehow magically become an enormously collaborative work of art.

KEY POINTS:

- Every production relies on the efforts of many "little people" to bring it to fruition.

- Even while a film may have thousands of people listed in the credits, the efforts of many will still go uncredited.

- Film is arguably the most collaborative art form.

- The greatest contribution of producers and directors is their ability to get many people to work together.

- "Above-the-line" talent refers to creatives like actors and directors whose pay is flexible, while "below-the-line" professionals have technical responsibilities and fixed salaries.

- Films are unlike most other consumer products because they are only created once by a large group of artists.

- The process of creating a film is, for the most part, standardized for the sake of efficiency.

- At every stage of the filmmaking process, there's something holding up progress.

- Each professional must show up prepared, and not interfere with the work of others.

- The creation of a film passes through three phases: production, distribution, and exhibition.

- Film production companies can be independent or are owned and operated by distributors.

- The film production has four stages: development, pre-production, production, and post-production.

- Development is the process of deciding to make a film.

- Pre-production is the process of planning a film.

- Production is the process of creating the elements that will make up the final film.

- Post-production is mainly the process of editing the film footage and other elements together.

9

CHAPTER TWO

THE CREATORS

In the movie, *Life of Pi* (2012), a young man, Pi Patel, is adrift at sea on a lifeboat with a Bengal tiger. When watching the film, the sense of isolation is palpable. In reality, the movie wasn't shot at sea, and there was no

Life of Pi (2012)

tiger. It was filmed in a water tank in Montréal, with dozens of crew members just out of camera range, and hundreds more creating the tiger with computer animation 4,500 miles away in Los Angeles. Ironically, in film, it takes a lot of people to create a sense of isolation.

It would be impossible to create a comprehensive list of jobs necessary for film production because each production is unique. However, it naturally follows that films with smaller budgets will have a smaller crew, because there is less money to hire people. Study the closing credits of any movie and you will get a true sense of how complicated film production is. Even those small-budget films require the work of many individuals.

The following is a list of common film production departments and jobs.

KEY CREATIVE TEAM

Producer

Producers have overall responsibility for assembling the elements that go into a film. A producer's role is usually more financial and practical than creative, but they might get involved in any stage of the production process. They will hire and oversee the above-the-line talent, but a producer's most important job is to secure funding, often from an executive producer. The producer's responsibilities are sometimes shared with co-producers or associate producers.

Director

The director is the figure usually perceived as a film's "artist" or "author." They have overall creative control and are specifically tasked with managing the actors' performances.

Screenwriter

The screenwriter creates the screenplay for a film, sets down the narrative and provides guidance about the story. There are numerous types of screenwriting credits such as "Story by," or "Adapted by," etc., but fundamentally, there is always a writer responsible for the script.

PRODUCTION DEPARTMENT

Executive Producer

An executive producer secures the funding for a film or has ownership of the intellectual property on which the film is based. The executive producer may have some creative control but is usually removed from the actual production process.

Line Producer

The line producer is the only below-the-line staff position recognized by the Producers Guild of America. The line producer reports directly to the producer and has the primary responsibility for the logistics of the production. They begin work in pre-production and continue until the filming has wrapped. As most of their work is done on set, they usually don't work in post-production. The line producer oversees budgets, contracts, union requirements, human resource-related issues, insurance, safety, and all on-set financial decisions.

Unit Production Manager

The unit production manager works closely with the line producer, and sometimes a single person will fill both roles. The unit production manager is the highest below-the-line staff position recognized by the Directors Guild of America and is responsible for overseeing the practical elements of production including shooting schedules. In non-DGA productions this position may be referred to as a "production manager" or "production supervisor." The unit production manager's primary job is to fulfill the vision of the director as efficiently as possible. Like the line producer, the unit production manager is responsible for staying within budget, but while the line producer is focused on not over-spending, the unit production manager is concerned with getting the greatest value for the money spent.

Assistant Production Manager

Assistant production managers assist the unit production manager and will most likely be assigned to oversee a specific department.

Chapter Two – The Creators

Production Coordinator

The production coordinator (sometimes referred to as a production office coordinator - POC) works under the unit production manager to coordinate all of the departments involved in production. The duties of a POC can be wide-ranging but are largely clerical in nature.

First Assistant Director

The first assistant director is the main aide to the director. The first assistant director works closely with the unit production manager and second assistant director(s) to make sure the director's wishes are executed. The first AD will also prepare the "day out of day" schedules and call sheets for the cast and crew, and ensure the documents are distributed.

Second Assistant Director

The second assistant director is the first A.D.'s assistant, and will manage background action, extras and some production assistants. The second AD works with the first AD to write and distribute daily production reports, end-of-day paperwork, notes for the next day, and call sheets, and the second AD also prepares and distributes script changes. On large productions, there may be more than one second AD.

Second Unit Director

The second unit is responsible for capturing establishing shots, insert shots, certain stunt sequences, and other shots that require a director, but not necessarily the main director's influence. The second unit director has creative control of the second unit.

Associate Producer

Typically, associate producers are the producer's assistants. However, at times this title has been abused and given in lieu of payment to anyone who has helped a production in a small way.

Production Assistant

Production assistants, or PAs, are general-purpose assistants to the production.

SCRIPT DEPARTMENT

Script Supervisor or Continuity Person

The script supervisor or continuity person (a position formerly known as the continuity girl) has a critical role in making sure that a film can be seamlessly edited together. Remarkably, the script supervisor is the only person in the script department. The script supervisor not only makes sure that the script is followed but that each shot will go together in terms of lighting, costumes, makeup, and action. This is particularly critical when a film is being shot out of sequence or when a scene must be reshot for technical reasons. The script supervisor will take photos and copious notes on the set to make sure everything is consistent and will also time the scenes, so the director and editors will have a better idea on how to cut the film.

PERFORMERS

Actor

Actors portray the characters created by the writer.

Stunt Performer

Stunt performers stand in for actors when a character must accomplish something especially dangerous.

Background Performer

Background performers (sometimes called extras) portray background characters, effectively becoming part of the set dressing.

Stand-ins

Stand-ins are generally not seen in the final film. They look and dress like the main characters and will take their place while lighting and camera movements are being worked out. Once filming starts, the stand-ins will step out and the actors will step in.

LOCATION DEPARTMENT

Location Manager / Scout

The location manager is responsible for researching and photographing potential filming locations. The location manager will also locate areas to park equipment trucks, identify access to power and other utilities, help secure the necessary permits in coordination with the production manager, and manage the location while filming is in progress.

Location Assistant

The location assistant is the first and last person on-set, facilitating the film crew's presence and cleaning up after them. The location assistant makes sure that the film crew's use of the location runs smoothly.

CAMERA DEPARTMENT

Director of Photography

The director of photography or "DP" works closely with the director in supervising the operation of the camera including focus, exposure, and movement. They also dictate lighting. The director of photography is sometimes known as the cinematographer, though some professionals insist that the term only applies when a single person functions as both the director of photography and the camera operator.

Camera Operator

The camera operator is the person responsible for the camera and camera crew. Modern cameras can be very complex, and are often run via computer, but they will still sometimes need several assistants to operate them.

Chapter Two – The Creators

First Assistant Camera

The job of the first assistant camera is to aid in operating the camera. They are sometimes called the "focus puller." The focus puller is responsible for adjusting the focus as the camera or the action in front of the camera moves during the scene. Computers can be used to pull focus sometimes, but because actors may not do precisely the same thing on each take, the focus may have to be adjusted manually. The first assistant camera also assembles, disassembles, and cleans the camera and equipment at the beginning and end of a day of shooting.

Second Assistant Camera

The second assistant camera assists the first assistant camera. They also use the clapperboard, or slate, to mark the beginning of each shot, and are responsible for arranging the loading and transportation of camera equipment.

Digital Imaging Technician

The digital imaging technician (DIT) is responsible for transferring data from the camera's memory to hard drives and making numerous back-ups. They will also distribute the copies in the appropriate resolution for review by the key creative and post-production teams. They must make sure that the software is up to date, functioning, and free from any viruses. When film was (or is) used, a similar role would have been fulfilled by the second assistant cinematographer / loader. The 2nd AC would carefully load unexposed film into magazines in a completely dark room. The magazines would be placed on the camera for filming, and then the exposed film was unloaded in a dark room and put into canisters for shipping to the lab.

Steadicam Operator

Steadicam is a brand name for a device that enables handheld cinematography with minimized camera-shaking. The Steadicam operation can be physically challenging. It often involves moving in a choreographed fashion while manipulating a camera that is harnessed to an operator looking at a display screen. The effect is mainly achieved by shifting the camera's center of gravity and not by gyroscopes or computers. The Steadicam operator will usually be assisted by a second operator who will control the focus and zoom by remote control. Because this is a specialized skill, it is not usually done by the regular camera operator.

Motion Control Technician/Operator

The motion control technician operates a motion control rig, a robotic device designed to repeat camera movements for special effects.

SOUND DEPARTMENT

Production Sound Mixer

The production sound mixer oversees the sound department on set and is responsible for all sound recording. This involves choosing the appropriate microphones, the operation of sound recording devices, and mixing audio in real-time.

Boom Operator

The boom operator is responsible for holding boom microphones – a microphone on a long pole – just outside of the frame to capture sound. While small wireless lavalier microphones are more effective than ever, the quality of sound from a boom microphone is still considered far superior.

GRIP DEPARTMENT

Grips

Grips are responsible for all camera and lighting rigging such as dollies and light stands.

Key Grip

The key grip works with the director of photography and oversees the other grips.

Best Boy Grip

The best boy grip is the main assistant to the key grip and has the responsibility to maintain all grip equipment.

ELECTRICAL DEPARTMENT

Gaffer/Chief Lighting Technician

The Gaffer implements the lighting design. The term likely comes from lamplighters who lit natural gas streetlamps in the 19th century. They would use a long stick with a hook called a "gaff" to light the lamps. Eventually, anyone who worked with lighting was called a gaffer.

Best Boy Gaffer

The gaffer's best boy is the gaffer's lead assistant. The best boy gaffer is responsible for maintaining all lighting equipment as well as supervising other lighting technicians.

Electrician

Electricians work closely with the lighting crew but handle the electrical set-up for the production, including power supply.

ART DEPARTMENT

Production Designer

The production designer works to fulfill the director's artistic vision. They are responsible for creating the physical visual appearance of the film including settings, costumes, props, and character makeup. The production designer is the head of the art department and along with the director of photography, and costumer to create the look of the film.

Art Director

The art director oversees the artists and craftspeople on the film crew to bring the production designer's vision to fruition.

Illustrator

The illustrator creates drawings for the production designer to be used as a guide for other artistic positions.

Set Decorator

The set decorator selects, designs, sources and creates all furniture and decorations on the film set that are in the background.

Buyer

The buyer locates, and then purchases or rents items for the set decorator.

Leadman

The leadman assists the set decorator and is the head set-dresser.

Set Dressers

The set dressers place the decorations on the set. As a group, they are sometimes called the "swing team" because they will swing into action before filming starts to put everything in place, and then swing into action again to strike it all when filming completes.

Greensman

The greensman is responsible for all plant material on the set.

Chapter Two – The Creators

Construction Coordinator

Orders materials, creates work schedules, and supervises the carpenters, painters and other scenery technicians.

Key Scenic

The key scenic is supervises the paint crew.

Prop Master / Propmaker

The prop master will supervise assistants to procure or build any object that is featured prominently in a film. During filming, they will also attend to consumable props such as food or cigarettes.

Weapons Master/Armorer

The weapons master or armorer is dedicated to safely acquiring and managing all weapons used in a production.

HAIR AND MAKEUP DEPARTMENT

Key Makeup Artist

The key makeup artist designs and supervises all make-up for a film.

Special Makeup Effects Artist

The special makeup effects artist applies prosthetics and other makeup-related practical effects.

Hair Stylist

Hair stylists style and maintain the hair and wigs of all the performers, being particularly careful that hair length is consistent throughout filming.

WARDROBE DEPARTMENT

Costume Designer

The costume designer conceives of the clothing worn in a film.

Costume Supervisor

The costume supervisor, formerly called the wardrobe supervisor, assists the costume designer and manages both the creation of new costumes and the purchase or rental of costumes. The costume supervisor will oversee cutter / fitters, jewelers, and textile artists.

Cutter / fitter

Cutter / fitters gather materials and construct the costumes per the designer's specifications. They will also fit and dress all performers including background performers.

Textile Artist

A textile artist will source and alter cloth as called for by the costume designer. They will also "distress" garments to make them appear dirty, faded and worn.

MISCELLANEOUS CREW

Casting Director

The casting director is responsible for creating character description breakdowns and casting calls, liaising with talent agents, running auditions, and hiring actors.

Storyboard Artist

The storyboard artist sketches comic book-like sequential drawings in pre-production (either with pen and paper, computer, or both) that will visualize for the director and cinematographer what each shot will look like.

Production Still Photographer

Production still photographers take pictures to be released for promotional materials, but their work can also assist in documenting the production for legal or historical purposes.

Documentary Videographer

The documentary videographer takes film footage of the production to be used in "making of" films and "behind-the-scenes" features for publicity purposes.

Unit Publicist

The unit publicist is the link between the film production and the media for the duration of the production stage. The unit publicist creates press releases,

releases publicity photographs, and facilitates interview requests.

Production Accountant

The production accountant will be responsible for all budgets and bookkeeping on a production, including accounts receivable, accounts payable, payroll, taxes, and other financial reports.

Legal Counsel

If a production has a resident lawyer, they will often be credited as the "legal counsel," or "attorney of business and legal affairs." Many attorneys will be involved in the production process behind the scenes protecting the rights of filmmakers, making deals, or working on compliance and clearance issues.

Stunt Coordinator

The stunt coordinator plans and arranges the performance of stunts, including the casting of stunt performers.

Animal Wrangler

Animal wranglers often need to be licensed by local authorities and are responsible for the care and training of any animals involved in a production.

Transportation Coordinator

The transportation coordinator oversees the transportation requirements for the film. In cooperation with the location manager, the transportation coordinator plans and maneuvers all the equipment trucks for the optimal efficiency of the production. The transportation coordinator is also responsible for arranging transportation and / or parking for the cast and crew.

Caterer and Craft Services

Catering is provided by specialized companies who drive catering trucks packed with food and a range of equipment including ovens, refrigerators, and tables & chairs to each set location. Union rules demand a full meal every six hours. In between, craft services (often referred to as "crafty") will provide a wide array of snacks and beverages.

Unit Nurse

On large productions, it's important to have a nurse on hand for first aid. Even the safest set can be a dangerous workplace because everything is rigged temporarily. It isn't like a factory setting, where safety measures can be routine. Each day the set can present new dangers.

Security Manager

The security manager will ensure the safety and security of the set and crew. If a film is on location for days, the expensive set and equipment are vulnerable, and any sort of criminal act can cause major delays. It is also critical to keep onlookers and fans from disrupting work on the set.

POST-PRODUCTION

Post-Production Supervisor

The post-production supervisor picks up where the line producer leaves off and is responsible for coordinating the post-production process, including the maintenance of communication between the producer, editor, supervising sound editor, facilities companies (such as film labs, CGI studios, and negative cutters) and the production accountant.

Visual Effects Producer

The visual effects producer is the project manager for all visual effects, the process by which imagery is created or manipulated outside the context of a live action shot in filmmaking. The role is similar to what the unit production manager does on the set. The duties of the visual effects producer can vary widely depending on the production, but the main challenge is to keep things on time and on budget while meeting the approval of the design team.

Sound Designer

The sound designer is responsible for adding sound not captured on location to a film's final cut. This includes dialogue, Foley, and music.

Sound Editor

The sound editor assembles and places all of a film's sound effects.

Re-Recording Mixer

The re-recording mixer balances all of a film's sounds for the final soundtrack.

Music Supervisor

The music supervisor helps integrate a film's music into the soundtrack and negotiates with the recording industry for music rights and usage.

Dialogue Editor

The dialogue editor is responsible for assembling and editing all dialogue in the soundtrack. They might also record and edit supplemental dialogue such as background conversations (sometimes referred to as "group loop") or re-record dialogue that was unusable from the on-set recording (referred to as ADR - Automatic Dialogue Replacement).

Composer

The composer writes a film's score in coordination with the director and the rest of the design team.

Foley Artist

The Foley artist creates sound effects for a film, using a variety of items to imitate what something on-screen should sound like.

Film Editor

The film editor, often with the help of several assistant editors, assembles the shots of a film, into the final film. Editing can be a tedious process and the personal style of an editor can greatly affect the final outcome of the film. However, sometimes the editor will be required to tightly follow to the storyboards that were created in pre-production. The director will often work with the editor on the final cut.

Negative Cutter

In productions shot on film, a negative cutter will splice together a film as directed by the editor and send it for the final prints to be made.

Colorist

When film is used, the colorist is responsible for color grading (formerly called color timing) using either chemical or digital processes to add and adjust a film's color, particularly so that the colors match from shot to shot.

Special Effects Supervisor

The special effects supervisor coordinates with all of designers and artisans (the prop makers in particular) to create all of the practical effects in a film. This might include models or pyrotechnic effects.

Visual Effects (VFX) Creative Director

The VFX creative director oversees production design for computer-generated elements of a film.

Chapter Two – The Creators

Visual Effects Supervisor

The visual effects supervisor leads the visual effects crew and works with the VFX creative director and the director to create computer images that support the film's desired look.

Visual Effects Editor

The visual effects editor incorporates the computer-generated objects into the live-action scenes to create a combined image.

Compositor

The compositor combines images from several different varieties of filming and animation to create a coherent look.

Rotoscope/Paint Artists

Rotoscope and paint artists add or remove details from a scene on a frame-by-frame basis.

Animator

Animators most often work on cartoons, but now more than ever they can be used to seamlessly add drawn images into the film. Typically, animation is now done via computer.

KEY POINTS:

- Hundreds or even thousands of people might be involved in a film production.

- Productions will vary significantly in which roles need to be filled, but most positions are critical to a successful production.

- While it will vary from production to production, typically there are 14 production departments: The Key Creative Team, Production Department, Script Department, Performers, Location Department, Camera Department, Sound Department, Grip Department, Electrical Department, Art Department, Hair and Makeup Department, Wardrobe Department, Miscellaneous Crew, Post-Production.

- The key creative team includes: the producer, the director, and screenwriter.

- The production department includes: the executive producer, the line producer, the unit production manager, the assistant production manager, the production coordinator, the first assistant director, the second assistant director, the second unit director, and the production assistants.

- There is only one person working in the script department, the script supervisor.

- Performers include actors, stunt actors, background actors, and stand-ins.
- Members of the location department include the location manager / scout and the location assistant.
- The camera department consists of the director of photography (or cinematographer), the camera operator, the first assistant camera, the second assistant camera, the digital imaging technician, the steadicam operator, and the motion control technician / operator.
- The sound department includes the production sound mixer and the boom operator.
- Members of the grip department include grips, the key grip, and the best boy grip.
- The electrical department consists of the gaffer / chief lighting technician, the best boy gaffer and the electricians.
- The art department consists of the production designer, the art director, the illustrator, the set decorator, buyers, the leadman, set dressers, greensmen, the construction coordinator, the key scenic, the prop master / propmaker, and the weapons master / armorer.
- The hair and make-up department is made up of the key makeup artist, the

special makeup effects artist, and hair stylists.

- The wardrobe department includes the costume designer, the costume supervisor, cutter / fitters, and textile artists.

- Among the miscellaneous crew are, the casting director, the storyboard artist, the production still photographer, the documentary videographer, the unit publicist, the production accountant, legal counsel, the stunt coordinator, animal wranglers, the transportation coordinator, the caterer and craft services, the unit nurse, and the security manager.

- The post-production staff includes the post-production supervisor, the visual effects producer, the sound designer, the sound editor, the re-recording mixer, the music supervisor, the dialogue editor, the composer, Foley artists, the film editor, negative cutters, colorists, the special effects supervisor, the visual effects creative director, the visual effects supervisor, the visual effects editor, compositor rotoscope / paint artists, and animators.

CHAPTER THREE

PRODUCING

"Have your people call my people and we'll do lunch" has been a Hollywood cliché for more than 50 years, but for producers, two or three power lunches per day can be a reality. And if each of the more than 7,000 members in the Producers' Guild ate two lunches per day every day . . . well that's a lot of bean sprouts.

The names of most producers are unfamiliar to audiences, and there's no Academy Award for "best producer." However, when a film wins an Oscar for "Best Picture," it's the producer who steps up to accept the award. After all, the producer is ultimately responsible for the final product.

Italian film producer, Dino De Laurentiis said:

"If no producer, no movie . . . The producer choose the story, choose the script writer, choose the director. Together with director, selects the cast. Stay in charge of production on time, stay in charge of postproduction, decide when the picture will be released, marketing and so on. If the picture is successful, the producer share the credit with everybody. If the picture is a flop, the only responsibility is the producer. Nobody else. Even if the director make a mistake, problem is the producer, he choose the wrong director."[1]

Dino De Laurentiis

There are some well-known producers, such as Stephen Spielberg or Ron Howard, but they're usually famous for other things like directing or acting. Other names like David O. Selznick or Samuel Goldwyn may be vaguely familiar to audiences, but for the most part, producers work quietly behind the scenes.

Producers are primarily businesspeople, and many have MBAs and years of experience in business. The job requires a lot of networking, negotiating, and convincing people to part with their money. Producers must also understand the filmmaking process and have a firm grasp of the legal intricacies of show business contracts. However, there are no explicit educational requirements to be a producer, so the only true barrier is knowing the right people.

Chapter Three – Producing

As Dino Di Laurentiis alluded to in the previous quote, the producer oversees all three phases necessary to bring a film to audiences: development, production, and distribution. Development is about the acquisition of talent, financing, and a distribution deal. Production is about the construction of the film. And distribution is about getting the film in front of an audience.

Development typically begins with a script. Either the producer will hire a screenwriter to create a script based on the producer's concept, or a screenwriter will pitch a script or story concept to the producer. If that happens, the producer will "option" the script. He will pay the writer a small sum to keep the script off the market for a year or so while he tries to "package" the film. Packaging a film is about getting all the key players and money into place.

At this point the producer will identify and collaborate with executive producers. Executive producers supply money, intellectual property (such as the right to adapt a book or the ownership of a franchise), collateral, or connections and a solid reputation for success.

Once a script has been selected and the executive producers are on board, the producer will hire the major talent, secure a distribution deal, and secure financing. Alternatively, in the case of a franchise, serial production, or sequel, it is possible that the talent, financing and distribution could precede the script.

Putting this all together is tricky. A producer needs financing to attract talent and get a distribution deal. However, a producer will also need to have the talent and distribution deal lined up before he can get financing. Getting the talent, distribution and financing to happen all at once relies on the reputation of the producer. Sometimes a producer will get the talent and distribution together but by the time they add the financing, the talent is no longer available. The producer then has to find new talent that will satisfy the financiers, but sometimes the new talent demands script changes and by the time that happens, the financing and distribution falls apart.

This process becomes a perpetual loop, called "development hell" and it can go on for many years. Eventually, the project gets a reputation for being toxic, and no one wants anything to do with it. This costs the producer a large sum of money and leaves him with a damaged reputation. It is possible to get bridge loans to avoid development hell, but the loans will only be given to a producer with an iron-clad reputation and significant collateral.

The development hell record is an astounding 79 years. In 1931, Looney Tunes' director, Robert Clampett first optioned Edgar Rice Burroughs's book, *A Princess of Mars*. The property would change hands many times but began production in 2010 and was ultimately released as the disappointing *John Carter* (2012).

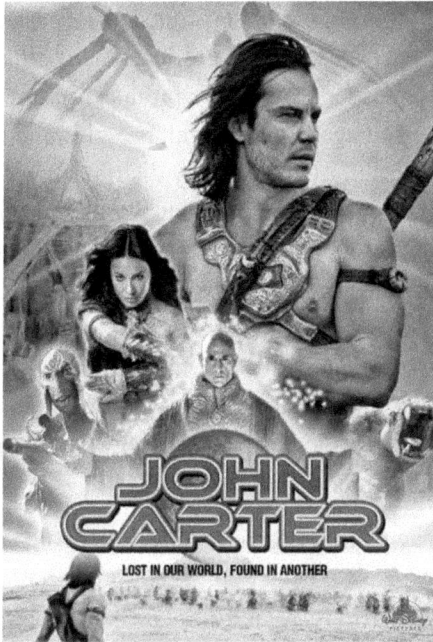

John Carter (2012)

Producers are gamblers, and like all gamblers they're lucky if they have as many successes as failures. Producers of small-budget independent films will suffer relatively minor losses and see modest gains, but independent films are also far more likely to have losses than profits. On the other hand, major Hollywood productions involve massively complex financing, and they can see enormous profits or losses, but a sophisticated producer of a large production is far more likely to see a profit than an independent film producer.

Of course, the wise producer will be gambling with someone else's money. Producers will often team up with equity partners (executive producers), but debt also can be financed against collateral, presales and minimum guarantees issued by trustworthy distribution companies, personal guarantees from high net-worth individuals, and property titles. Producers also seek the best tax advantages and currency exchange rates in order to minimize costs. Foreign countries and local communities will often offer incentives to bring production to their area. It will typically take from a year to a year and a half from the time a project is proposed to when it's packaged and gets the "green light".

When a film is greenlit, the project moves into the production phase. At this point, the producer will hire a line producer to create and monitor the budget through production, and a unit production manager who will oversee the project management of the production. The unit production manager will, in turn, hire assistant production managers to oversee each production department and a production coordinator to handle administrative production tasks.

Some producers may be working on several films at once and have them at various stages of production. This may keep them too busy to be deeply involved in the production stage. On the other hand, some producers prefer to be in control at every stage. Likewise, some directors dislike producers micromanaging their work, while others believe that having the producer on the set is helpful.

The assistant directors and the second-unit director will be hired next, and the various crews will be contracted. What happens after that will vary dramatically based on the particular production, but typically principal shooting will take between three and four months.

The producer will have administrative control over a film and filmmakers but must also understand the creative aspects to make good judgement calls. Sometimes directors wish to keep producers at arm's length, so they won't interfere with the creative process. Other directors wish to have the producer heavily involved. They rely on the producer to handle all practical matters so they can focus on artistic choices.

It can be another ten months or more between the end of production and when the film premiers. This is called the post-production period, but in reality, post-production begins at the same time as production. As soon as principle shooting commences, the post-production supervisor will begin coordinating communication between the producer, editor, supervising sound editor, CGI studios, main title sequence and credits supervisors, and effect coordinators.

The producer will also work with the distributor through production and post-production to formulate a release strategy. They will consider the movie's genre, target audience, and conflicts with other films being released at the same time. For example, it may be best to release a horror film closer to Halloween and children's film in the summer. If a big tentpole blockbuster is going to be released on a given date, it may be better to wait for a slower week to release a smaller film. If the film is a contender for award nominations, it might be best to hold the release for later in the year, when it will still be fresh in the minds of the voting committees.

The producer will work with the distributor on marketing the film too. With the rise of social media, marketing has become more complex. The unit publicist, the production still photographer, and sometimes a social media coordinator will work through production to get a buzz going in the media. A documentary videographer will capture behind-the-scenes moments that can be used for archival purposes and for the press, as well as DVD bonus features. Meanwhile, other marketing efforts will be made to create and place movie trailers, advertisements, and theater signage, as well as product tie-ins with clothing manufacturers, toy companies, and restaurants. Publicists will be hired to communicate with reviewers and to create publicity events such as premiere nights.

In large productions, the producer's duties will be so wide-ranging that they need to be divided among co-producers, and typically some work also will be delegated to associate producers, who function as their assistants. Unfortunately, the associate producer title has been abused. Sometimes people will be given that credit in lieu of payment, even though they've contributed very little to the production. For example, the producer might want to give a relative the credit as a present, or perhaps someone who has helped secure a unique filming location (such as a military base or other secure location) will be named associate producer. This sort of thing happened more often than it should, and it was frowned upon by the Producers Guild of America.

Eventually, it became widely understood that the associate producer credit was meaningless. So those who gave out favors began asking for other types of producing credits. Soon those credits were handed out freely too. For example, the film, *Lee Daniels' The Butler* (2013) lists five producers, four co-producers, 20 executive producers, six co-executive producers, and six associate producers. That's 41 producers working on a film with a relatively modest budget ($30 million).

The PGA now has stringent rules about who can become a member of the guild, and they've implemented the "producers mark." The producers mark is the letters "p.g.a" after the producer's name in the credits. It signifies that the named person "performed a majority of the producing duties on the film." Unlike most other guild marks in a film's credits, it does not signify membership in the guild. It is simply a method of noting which of the many people with a producer credit had the greatest responsibility for the film. At this time, only theatrically released films will be eligible for this designation.

KEY POINTS:

- While the names of film producers may be unfamiliar to audiences, without them there would be no film.
- Producers are businessmen, but there are no particular qualifications necessary to be a producer.
- Having good connections to money and talent is critical for producers.
- Having a strong knowledge of business, law, and filmmaking is also helpful.
- A reputation for success is probably the most important asset of all.
- Producers will work on a film for years and see it through development, production (including pre-production, production, and post-production), and distribution.
- The process usually begins when a producer or executive producer options a script.
- Development is about bringing together a script, talent, financing, and a distribution deal.
- A project that has a hard time putting those things together is said to be in "development hell."
- Executive producers will provide money, influence, and / or ownership of intellectual property to the project.

- When all the development elements come together, the project gets "greenlit" and proceeds to production.
- The line producer is responsible for managing the budget.
- The unit production manager will oversee production and hire all the assistant production managers.
- Some directors dislike having the producer on the set for fear they will micromanage things, others welcome the help.
- Small budget films will typically see only small profits or losses, but it is more likely that they will lose money. Large budget films have the potential for huge profits or losses, but they are more likely to have a profit.
- In addition to securing equity partners, films can be financed against collateral, presales and minimum guarantees issued by trustworthy distribution companies, personal guarantees from high net-worth individuals, and property titles.
- Producers seek the best tax advantages and currency exchange rates in order to minimize costs.
- Production and post-production will begin at the same time.

- The unit production manager will be in charge of production, and the post-production supervisor coordinates post-production.
- The producer will also work with the distributor through production and post-production to formulate a release strategy.
- The producer will work with the distributor on marketing too.
- The producer's duties may be divided among co-producers.
- Some production work will be delegated to associate producers.
- The associate producer title is sometimes given out to people who have contributed very little.
- The Producers Guild of America has stringent rules about who can become a member of the guild.
- The "p.g.a" producers mark does not signify membership in the guild but indicates which person performed the majority of the producing duties.

CHAPTER FOUR

DIRECTING

It might seem reasonable to suggest that the job of a stage director and the job of a film director are similar, but this is not the case. In stage productions, the playwright creates the narrative and the goal of the director is to bring the playwright's vision to life. In film, the director creates the narrative, and the script is merely a tool used to tell that story. Actors in a stage play will vie for the audience's attention and maybe even upstage each other because the audience has free will over where they will focus their attention. In a film, the director controls what the audience will look at. Because the director is in control of everything that is seen and heard in a film, they are referred to as the "auteur" (French for "author") of the film.

A feature film director must be able to visualize and construct each of the roughly 160,000 frames that go into a film, and then marry them to a soundtrack in an orderly fashion to create a narrative. Doing so requires knowledge of each craft associated with film, as well as a firm understanding of storytelling principles. As a practical matter, the director must continually compare the present reality of the production with the vision he has for the film and make quick decisions to bring those two things to parity.

In 2002, director George Lucas put it this way:

"I'm stubborn and creative. Anybody who works in an artistic medium trying to create something does not like people looking over their shoulder going, 'No no no, make it blue! Make it green!' If you have a vision, you don't want a lot of outside influence. A director makes 100 decisions an hour. Students ask me how you know how to make the right decision, and I say to them, 'If you don't know how to make the right decision, you're not a director.' That's all there is to it. If you have to think about it, you can't direct something. There are directors out there who don't know how to make up their minds, but a true director has an idea in his head and can instantly weigh any decision against that and say, 'That's right, that's wrong.' You welcome feedback from talented people, not marketing people or executives who aren't creative."[2]

George Lucas

Sometimes directors get known for making a certain type of film. For example, Wes Craven was known for making horror films, Vincente Minnelli was known for musicals, and Alfred Hitchcock was known for suspense movies. Some directors focus on a genre by choice, but others just never get a chance to try something new. Occasionally an exceptional director will get the opportunity to defy expectations and work in many genres. For example, Billy Wilder's filmography includes courtroom drama, farce, romance, war, noir, musical, documentary and more.

Because a film is a product of its director's vision, it will bear the idiosyncrasies of its creator. Woody Allen films are distinctly different from Robert Altman films. And Rob Reiner films are distinctly different from Sam Peckinpah or Frank Capra films, and so on. Because of this, a producer will be very careful to pair the script with an appropriate director.

On a big-budget film, this might be the most important decision a producer will make. This may mean that the producer will choose someone with significant experience or someone that they have worked with before. However, producers sometimes prefer younger directors, not only because they have enthusiasm and a fresh perspective, but because they are easier to manipulate. Without a reputation for success, a young director will be forced to defer to the producer's demands. Sometimes directors will write and produce their own films so they can maintain complete control. For example, James

Cameron has been the writer, director, and producer on more than a dozen films.

It's notable that only 9% of big-budget films are directed by women.[3] Given that a director's viewpoint, style, and idiosyncrasies fundamentally shape a film, it's reasonable to suggest that the gender of the director will make a significant difference in the final product.

There are many competing theories as to why there are fewer female directors. Some suggest that because the target audience for movies is 25-34-year-old males, so it makes sense that a producer would seek out a male director. However, while it is true that men in that age range see an average of 4 films per person, and women in that demographic only see 3.5 films per person, 51% of all moviegoers are female. Perhaps if there were more female directors, they would see more movies.[4]

It may be that women are less inclined to compete aggressively with their male counterparts to win directing jobs, choosing instead to make smaller independent films. However, the most likely answer is that Hollywood remains an "old boys" network where producers (most of whom are male) feel more comfortable working with male directors. When Kathryn Bigelow became the first woman to win the Best Director Academy Award for *The Hurt Locker* (2008), there was optimism that this would lead not only to more women directing major films but more women directing big-budget action films. So far, this has not been the case.

Kathryn Bigelow

Directors are above all else storytellers, but they have many more practical duties that are critical to a production's success. Directors must be leaders and project managers because they create their stories in cooperation with many other artisans. They must keep the production on schedule and within budget. They must delegate authority and refrain from micromanagement, but they must also have the knowledge to communicate with actors, designers, cinematographers, and technicians. At times they may need to be artists, musicians, choreographers, or psychologists. Directors must be able to mediate differences in creative vision and command the respect of those they are leading.

The role of the director is much like that of a conductor or athletic coach. While they don't necessarily have complete authority in the filmmaking process

53

(particularly when it comes to business decisions) everyone looks to them for cohesion and guidance. It's the responsibility of the director to motivate everyone involved with the production and to arbitrate any conflicts that arise. Some directors will be very authoritarian, but perhaps the best directors will inspire confidence with a steady, unflappable disposition.

Making motion pictures is not like making consumer packaged goods that roll off an assembly line day after day. Every film and film production process is unique. It brings together a team of people, who often have never worked with each other before, to solve problems that they may never have faced before. Film production relies on the professionalism of filmmakers who know their craft and are prepared for anything. Filmmaking also relies on a standard vocabulary and processes to help eliminate communication problems, but when the unexpected happens, it is up to the director to smooth things over.

While smaller productions tend to be simpler in terms of project management, they're often made by people with less experience, performing multiple jobs, under less-than-perfect conditions. Big budget films can be logistical nightmares, and because of the cost, they must be completed at a lightning pace. Regardless of the production, at any given moment, there's always something keeping things from proceeding, and it's up to the director to get things moving forward again. This makes directing a very stressful job.

The key to reducing that stress is to prepare well in the preproduction process, and one of the most important jobs for the director during preproduction is to create a "shooting script." Most screenplays begin as a "spec script" intended to sell the idea to a producer. A shooting script, on the other hand, will often specify every camera movement and edit as well as a thorough description of characters, sets, costumes, locations, effects, titles, and so on. During the preproduction process, the director will work with the writers and other artistic personnel to create the shooting script.

The director will also create a character "breakdown" (description of casting needs) in preproduction, and work with the casting director, and producers to create audition scripts, and schedule and hold auditions. Directors will also conduct "read-throughs" and rehearsals in the preproduction period.

The director will plan the overall look of the film with production designers and the director of photography in the preproduction process. And they will work with a storyboard artist to draw a sketch for each shot in the film, resulting in a sort of comic book instruction manual for the movie.

Directors must communicate with producers on budgets, permits, equipment rental, contracts, union issues, the shooting schedule, and so on, but typically directors will delegate much of that decision making to others. Some directors feel that being meticulously prepared in the preproduction process makes the filming go more smoothly and ensures that everyone is working toward a common goal. Other directors feel that over-preparation wastes time and eliminates spontaneity in the filming process.

Almost all the artistic choices are made by the time production begins. The necessary elements will have been gathered and prepared, and now it's time to put them before the camera. At this point, the director will split most of his time between coaching the actors and conferring with the director of photography. There will be others to oversee things like logistics, set decoration, transportation, wardrobe, background performers and so on. A good director will resist micromanaging others but will still want to maintain control over every element of production to maintain his artistic vision. The director will also continue to coordinate with the producer to make sure that everything is on time and on budget. As filming proceeds, the director will review and determine which takes should be used by the editor in postproduction.

In postproduction, the director will supervise the addition of music and sound effects. Sometimes additional dialogue will be recorded too. Then the editing process can begin.

An editor will make a rough cut, the first pass at putting the film together, and then the director and editor will work on the second edit, which is sometimes called the director's cut. The third and final edit is done under the supervision of the producer, who will mostly be concerned with length, contractual obligations (such as an actor's screen time or product placement), achieving a particular MPAA rating, possible intellectual property violations, adjustments in response to test audiences, and so on.

Occasionally the director's cut will be released at a later date as a way of appeasing fans who suspect the producers are censoring the director's art. However, these so-called director's cuts are usually a fourth cut of the film ordered by the producer to help sell additional copies of the movie and have nothing to do with the director's wishes. These "director's cuts" often merely reintroduce deleted scenes that were deemed unnecessary and slowed the pace of the film.

In most cases in the United States, films are owned by the producers because directors are employed on a "work-for-hire" basis. Directors can be fired and replaced at any time. So even while the director is considered the "author" of the film, the producer owns the intellectual property. This means that unless otherwise stipulated in a contract, producers get the last word on what is seen in a film and can alter the film in any way for future releases. In some other countries, the director has the final authority over the film's content, and it cannot be altered without the director's consent.

Of course, the role of the director will likely be entirely different on small budget films and documentaries, where a team of people will collaborate more closely and often take on multiple roles. In that case, the director might also be the producer, writer, director of photography, or editor. Working with a smaller crew certainly simplifies communication, and simplicity helps mitigate a smaller budget.

Beyond work on the actual film, directors can play a role in the distribution stage. Since they are perceived by the public as the creators of the films, they can be useful in giving interviews and marketing a film. While some directors believe that a good film should require no explanation, others are delighted to talk about the process because it serves to build their personal brand.

The amount of credit and blame that directors receive for their films is not entirely unwarranted. Their importance may be somewhat inflated, but it should not be understated either. Still, while it is convenient to imagine a film as having a single author, it is important to remember that the director's main role is to coordinate and supervise all the other professionals who make a film come together.

KEY POINTS:

- The director is the auteur (author) of the film.
- Directors control everything that is seen and heard in a film.
- Directors must be quick decision-makers.
- Films bear the idiosyncrasies of their directors.

- Hiring the right director for the script is one of the producer's most important decisions.
- Sometimes producers want to hire an experienced director, but they sometimes prefer a young competent director who will yield to their demands.
- Some directors prefer to write and produce their own stories so they can have complete control.
- Despite the unique perspective women can bring to films, they remain under-represented in the field of directing.
- Directors are above all else storytellers.
- Directors are responsible for coordinating and motivating everyone involved in the filmmaking process.
- Every production is different and comes with different challenges, and it falls to the director to guide the cast and crew through these challenges.
- Small productions may be easier to manage, but more of the responsibility will fall on the director.
- Directing is stressful because there is always something holding up the production, and it's the director's job to get things moving again.
- A significant part of the director's job occurs in preproduction.

- Some directors prefer to craft very careful plans before they begin filming, while others favor a more spontaneous style.
- Directors will oversee the creation of character breakdowns, auditions, casting, read-throughs, and rehearsals.
- Directors will collaborate to convert the spec script into a shooting script.
- The director will plan the overall look of the film with production designers and storyboard artists.
- During production, the director is usually the highest authority on-set but will spend most of the time supervising the actors and cinematographer.
- In postproduction, the director will supervise the addition of music, sound effects, and additional dialogue.
- The director works with the editor to create the second cut (the "director's cut") of a film before the producer takes control for the final cut.
- In the United States, producers own the intellectual property and have the final say on what is seen in a film. In other countries, the director has the final authority over the film, and it cannot be altered without his consent.

- Directors are also involved in marketing and publicity for their films due to the general perception of them as the films' creators.
- Directors must be talented both at storytelling and at project management.

CHAPTER FIVE

ACTING

Actors are the highest-profile professionals in the film industry. They're the center of attention both on- and off-screen. Actors (in the guise of their characters) drive the narrative, and audiences vicariously take the journey with them. Together, audiences and the characters struggle with the heroes and work to defeat the villains.

It's no wonder that audiences feel a special connection to actors. It's as if they know them personally. Further, audiences are also apt to confuse the actors with the characters they play and imagine them to behave similarly in real life. On the other hand, actors feel like they don't know the audience at all. In fact, they sometimes barely know their scene partner.

In the early days of movies, actors wanted nothing to do with film. Serious stage actors in the 19th century were prized for their ability to interpret great dialogue and hold the rapt attention of large audiences for hours. Silent film had little dialogue, and there was no audience present during the filming. Film acting didn't require the endurance of stage acting, and if a mistake was made, the scene could simply be reshot. This could hardly be construed as acting. In fact, the earliest films showed "real" people in everyday life and didn't use actors at all.

In the early twentieth century, things began to change. Film became more narrative, and production moved to southern California, far from the great stage actors in New York City. Even when stage actors journeyed across the continent to try their luck in film, they found that their stage acting style didn't translate well to the new medium. The exaggerated expressions and gestures that worked well on stage looked absurd when the camera came in close, and comedians found it difficult to time their jokes with no feedback from a live audience. In time, some actors like Douglas Fairbanks and Charlie Chaplin mastered the craft and they were among the first movie stars. Indeed, as the fame of film stars spread across the country, more actors came to master their craft in Hollywood.

Douglas Fairbanks, Sr. in *The Thief of Bagdad* (1924)

Chapter Five - Acting

When sound came to film in the 1930s the ability to speak well and sing became mandatory for actors. This drew more serious actors to the screen and film acting became a distinct craft. By the 1950s, acting schools began to train actors for the unique demands of film.

There are many styles of acting. Some of the most well-known are Stanislavski's System ("The System"), the Strasberg Method ("Method Acting"), the Meisner Technique, and Practical Aesthetics. There are also many famous actor training programs in the U.S. such as The Actor's Studio, Second City, The Pasadena Playhouse, Julliard, The Actor's Conservatory Theatre, and The Theatre School at DePaul University. There are also many great foreign acting programs such as the National Institute of Dramatic Art in Kensington, Australia and the Oxford School of Drama in the UK. Each technique, school, and geographical region will produce actors with a slightly different style.

However, actors all have one major thing in common; when the director says, "action," they do something. They take action. Doing something is at the heart of acting. Acting is not about feelings. Actors don't think in emotional terms. Yes, the character they're playing may be sad, or happy, or hungry, or full of lust, but an actor is more concerned about what they're going to do about those feelings. In fact, for the most part, actors react more than they act. When an actor asks a director "what their motivation is," they want to know what they are supposed to be reacting to.

Some people believe that actors are great at pretense, but an actor will say that their job is about telling the truth. Pretty much everything in film is fake, but an actor wants everything he does to be honestly motivated. It is an actor's job to find truth in a universe of phoniness.

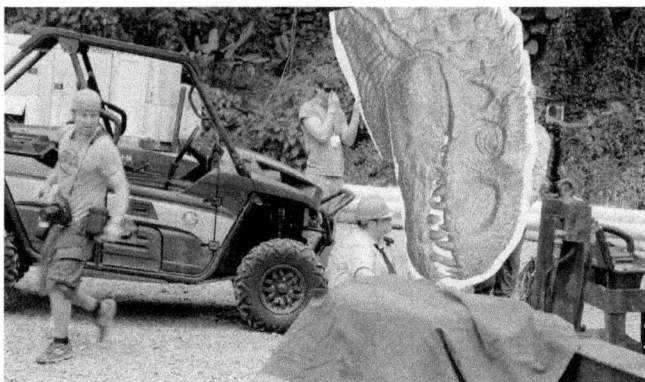

Eric Edelstein and production assistants on the set of *Jurassic World* (2015).

On stage, acting is a long series of reactions from the beginning of the play to the end. In a film, the character's motivation may not be so clear to an actor. This is because films are often shot out of sequence, or perhaps they're motivated by an incident or an effect that will be added later. For example, in *Jurassic World* (2015), actor, Eric Edelstein, plays the supervisor of a dinosaur enclosure who gets eaten by an "indominous rex." Mr. Edelstein had to play the scene for the camera without the benefit (or perhaps the challenge) of facing a real dinosaur because that animated effect was added in postproduction. The crew framed the shot using a cardboard cutout of the beast, but when it came time to film the shot the cardboard was removed. Mr. Edelstein had to imagine himself being eaten while being mindful to stay in the frame and imagine the visual and sound effects that would be added later. It's not nearly as easy as it looks.

Close-up shots can also be a challenge. In the final film, an audience might see a character having an intimate conversation with someone. When the close-up is being filmed however, the actor will more likely be staring into the face of the director or the director of photography than their scene partner.

Birdman or (The Unexpected Virtue of Ignorance) (2014)

For example, in *Birdman or (The Unexpected Virtue of Ignorance)* (2014) the central character, Riggan, is talking to other characters sitting across from him in a theater dressing room. From a production still, it can be seen that it was actually the director and director of photography who were sitting there. A Steadicam operator is set to move around behind the actor, Michael Keaton, and the director and DP will be digitally removed from the final film and the characters Riggan is supposed to be talking to will be inserted. Often a scene partner isn't even in the room, and their lines are read by the script supervisor. This can require an enormous amount of concentration on the part of the actor, particularly if the production is running behind schedule or over-budget.

This can be even more challenging for the "day players." Day players are actors who are hired to play small roles, and typically only get one day of work on a film. Most actors and directors will tell you that they play a crucial role. If acting is really reacting, having a competent scene partner is critical. A day player must be able to convey who their character is and what they want, with a quick glance because that's all the screen time they'll get. The day player might not ever see the whole script and certainly won't have seen any of the other scenes being filmed. They wait patiently for hours in a cramped trailer but are then rushed to the set to do their part with little-to-no direction. While the crew might have some patience for a star who wants to rework things or hold up the production, no one will have patience for the day player doing so. Day players will usually make the minimum union wage and find themselves auditioning more than acting. Day players get very little respect, but almost everyone will agree they're an important part of any film.

Some actors become very adept at small roles. Frequently they have a physical presence or voice that's instantly recognizable. These are the "character actors." They tend to work more often than day players, because they've developed a reputation for being reliable, and frequently they will have more than one day on a shoot. For example, the very recognizable Charles Lane has 361 screen credits in a career that stretched from 1930 – 1995.

Charles Lane

Another unsung hero of the acting world is the "stand-in." Stand-ins are never seen in the final film, but they might work through the whole production. Stand-ins look very much like the central characters and will be costumed like them too. They will take the place of the lead actors while the lighting and cinematography are being worked out. Sometimes they stand around for hours while the shot is being perfected and then, when everything is finally right, they'll step out to let the lead actors take their positions.

"Body doubles" and "stunt performers" also stand in for main characters, but they are seen in the final film. This can often save a considerable amount of money. A body double might be used for extreme long shots or close-ups. For example, if a character plays a musical instrument in a scene, but the actor doesn't really know how to play, a body double might be used to show a close up of his hands. In *The Sting* (1973) card tricks that were performed by Paul Newman's character, Henry Gondorff, were actually executed by sleight-of-hand magician John Scarne. If there's an extreme long shot of a car driving down a road, it might be cheaper or easier to use a body double than have the lead actor driving. Body doubles are also used when actors are unavailable or when they are unable or unwilling to do nude scenes.

Stunt performers are used when the action of a scene is dangerous. Because there can be millions of dollars on the line, no production wants to shut down operations waiting for a lead actor to heal from an injury. In fact, insurance companies and lawyers generally won't even allow it anymore. Recently there has been an increased reliance on computer-generated stunts rather than physical effects. These can sometimes be very spectacular without requiring a stunt performer at all, but today's action films nevertheless keep stunt performers quite busy.

"Background performers" (also known as "extras") are actors who add to the atmosphere of crowd scenes. Really, they're more like set dressing or props than actors. The most important thing is that the background actors don't call attention to themselves. They are often hired en masse by specialized casting directors. Central Casting, for example, has famously specialized in casting extras in Hollywood since 1925. They will even supply stock costumes for their background actors. This is why when someone looks like a stereotype, people will say they look like they're "straight out of Central Casting." These days, films rarely use a cast of thousands, opting instead to use computer-generated "background performers" because they are certainly cheaper and more cooperative.

There are other types of film performers: animal performers, puppeteers, dancers, models, singers, narrators, and more. They may not have the skills of a trained actor, but they help to tell the story. In fact, with a greater emphasis on editing, special effects, and other filmic devices, filmmakers find they can tell compelling stories without relying heavily on the talents of actors.

An actor's life may seem glamorous, but it isn't easy. Like many others in the film industry, actors are independent contractors, and must constantly look for the next job. Unlike others in the industry, they are selling themselves. It's necessary that actors believe in themselves and have large egos because actors either face constant rejection or have the weight of a multi-million-dollar production resting on their talent.

KEY POINTS:

- Actors are the most high-profile professionals in film.
- Actors drive the narrative.
- Audiences perceive they have a close relationship with actors and often conflate the actors with the roles they play.
- Film actors, on the other hand, can feel disconnected from the audience.
- It was not until the 1920s before film acting became a distinct and respected craft.
- When sound became part of film, actors needed to create more nuanced performances.
- There are numerous actor training programs and styles.
- While acting is not about feelings or emotions, but about reacting to some motivation.
- Ironically, while virtually everything about a film is fake, actors focus on being honest.

- On stage, acting is a long series of reactions, but in film, an actor's motivation may not be present.
- Day players are actors who are hired to play small roles, and typically only get one day of work on a film.
- Character actors will work more frequently because they're reliable and have a distinct look.
- A stand-in will take the place of an actor while the technical aspects of a shoot are worked out.
- Body doubles and stunt performers will also take the place of actors when they cannot be present, when special skills are required, or when it is too dangerous for them to be there.
- Background performers (extras) function to give an authentic look to the background.
- There are many other kinds of performers in film, including animal performers, puppeteers, dancers, models, singers, and narrators.
- Actors are independent contractors who are constantly looking for the next job.
- Actors face constant rejection, but the success or failure of a multimillion-dollar film may rest on their talents.

CHAPTER SIX

SCREENWRITING

In the script for the classic *Sunset Boulevard* (1950), the central character, Joe Gillis, is asked if he's written any screenplays. "Sure have," he replies, "The last one I wrote was about cattle rustlers. Before they were through with it, the whole thing played on a torpedo boat." Screenwriters get no respect. Ironically, before Sunset Boulevard was finished the line was changed to "The last one I wrote was about Oakies in the Dust Bowl. Before they were through with it, the whole thing played on a torpedo boat."

Sunset Boulevard (1950)

Most productions begin with the script or at least a story idea. At that point, a good writer is considered vital, but by the end of production, there may be little left of the original screenplay and numerous people may have a hand in the rewrites. The final script will likely be written and shaped in part by the director, producer, and cinematographer. Actors will often ad lib during shooting, and editors may get the final word by cutting and rearranging the film. In the end, there are often thirty or more people who have a hand in creating the script, but most will never receive credit.

The Writers Guild of America (WGA) has a detailed 27-page manual on how to determine screenwriting credits for all major television and live-action films. When filming is complete producers are required to submit to the guild a list of proposed writing credits. If there is any disagreement or questions about the credits, the WGA arbitration committee will read all drafts of the script and any supporting material, and then make an official determination of how the credits will read. Because the producers and directors already have so much influence over the final film, they will not usually be given a writing credit unless they have obviously contributed substantially to the story or screenplay.

Writers for animation are not represented by the WGA. They're represented by The Animation Guild (TAG). This largely came about by happenstance. While both unions have roots that go back to the 1930s, TAG was formed in 1952, and the WGA was created in 1954.

As TAG was already representing animation writers, there was no reason to give up that control to the WGA. Further, until Disney produced the first animated feature film, *Snow White and the Seven Dwarfs* (1937), animation was often more a compilation of visual gags than a story. Historically, the line between writers and artists has always been blurry in animation. Today, this is compounded by the fact that the line between animation and live-action has blurred. For example, Walt Disney's animated *Aladdin* (1992) was created under a TAG contract and listed 20 writers. When Disney turned that same story into a live-action film *Aladdin* (2019) they used the same narrative and most of the dialogue, but only credited two writers, neither of whom worked on the original animation.

If the film is not adapted from another source, and the story and the script are a product of the same writer(s), the credit will be "written by." The "story by" credit is used when the story was written specifically for the film (not an adaptation) by a writer who did not also write the screenplay. This is considered the minimal credit for any writer(s) who created the original story. If the screenplay is only loosely based on another source the credit will read "screen story by." Rarely, the "adapted by" credit is used when the script closely follows the original source material. If two writers work together on a screenplay, their names will be joined with an "&," but if they worked on different drafts of the script, their names will be joined with an "and." In general, story and screenplay credits cannot be shared by more than two people. However, a writing team is considered a single author, so theoretically the credits could read something like, "Story by Eric Jones & Frank Riley and Megan Smith & Bill Thomas, Screenplay by Ellen Brown & Raj Harris and Malcolm Green & Toni Stein."

The most important skill a screenwriter possesses is the ability to tell a story. He must be an expert with things like theme, character, conflict, and dialogue. He must be skilled with comedy and tragedy and all other aspects of dramatic structure, but even that's not enough to be a great screenwriter.

Above all else, screenwriters have to be adept at marketing their story. No one will beat a path to a screenwriter's door to read his screenplay; so much of a screenwriter's job is selling that script. There are no strict "rules" about how one does that, but the process usually includes a synopsis, a story treatment, and a logline.

A synopsis is a brief – usually only a page long – summary of the story from beginning to end. The summary is written in standard narrative form.

Compare that to a story treatment. A treatment is usually around 40 pages (one-third the traditional length of a finished script), but the length varies widely. Again, there are no strict rules on this, but it should be just long enough to get the job done. The goal of the treatment is to tell the story scene-by-scene. It should describe all of the characters and the action in a narrative form.

Finally, the writer must create a logline. A logline is usually a one-sentence teaser describing the story. It might begin by identifying the story's genre, and then go on to describe the main characters and action of the story. For example, this is the logline for *The Godfather* (1972): "The Godfather is a crime drama about an aging patriarch of an organized crime dynasty transferring control of his clandestine empire to his reluctant son."

The Godfather (1972)

Armed with the synopsis, treatment, and logline, the screenwriter is ready to "pitch" his idea. The pitch might be directed at a producer, studio executive, agent, manager, investor, director, actor, or anyone else who might have the power to get a film produced. There are no rules for a pitch, but that's not the case with the screenplay itself.

A script is like a blueprint. It's a good idea to have a blueprint before building a house, but no one lives in a blueprint. Likewise, a production team has to have a script before they start making a movie, but no one is going to a cinema to see a script. It's a jumping-off point, but a screenplay is not the final product.

There are many rules for writing a screenplay, and it is necessary to adhere to them. Films require the collaboration of many people, and all of them will turn to the script for guidance. Just as a blueprint must contain all of the proper notations and measurements in standard units, a script must use standard terms and format, so it's easily read.

Scripts are typically 120 pages and are laid out in a three-act structure. The first act is about thirty pages long and will result in about a half-hour of screen time. This section will include most of the exposition. It will introduce all of the important characters, establish the main challenge for the central character, and prepare the central character for their journey.

The second act is sixty pages and will describe roughly an hour of screen time. This section builds the tension and adds complications to the journey. The end of the second act will often bring the central character to the point of no return. A central character may find himself in the lair of the antagonist and will have no choice but to battle his way out. This is not the climax of the story, but simply the moment of total commitment for the central character.

The third act is another 30 pages and the last half hour or so of screen time. Having committed to seeing the journey through to the end, the central character finds himself in an epic struggle that will lead to a climax at the end of the story.

This three-act structure might vary slightly in terms of pages and time, but that won't happen very often. Watching a film, it's usually easy to spot major transitions at 30 and 90 minutes into the film. This standard helps to keep the production on track, and over time, audiences have come to subconsciously expect these transition points, and it helps them appreciate the story.

It's also important for a screenplay to be "tight" and not overwritten. A good screenwriter will keep the script succinct. They must convey the story but allow the other artists (including the actors) and members of the production team the opportunity to have their own influence on the project. As film is a visual medium, it's best to let the visuals, and not the dialogue, tell the story. It's particularly painful when there's too much dialogue in the first act in an effort to put out copious exposition, or in the third act if the antagonist spends an inordinate amount of time explaining what actually happened in the story.

Sometimes, the basis for a screenplay is not the screenwriter's own device, but an adaption from another source, like a book, a comic, a TV show, or even an older film. This source material must necessarily be greatly altered before it can be a workable script. There are three main ways in which the material will be altered: elision, interpolation, and interpretation.

Elision is the act of collapsing, truncating, or contracting something. Most non-film media lack the time constraints of film. They can luxuriate in longer, more complex stories. In order to adapt them for the screen, the screenwriter must cut some of the story to keep the film to a reasonable length.

Interpolation is the process of changing a story's content for the sake of elision. While elision is simply the removing or compressing of narrative events, interpolation will actually alter the plot in order to make it work for film. For example, two characters might be merged into one to simplify the narrative, or subplots might be simplified so they don't distract from the main plot. While it represents a more radical change than elision, interpolation is still focused on simplifying the source material.

West Side Story (1961)

Interpretation is when a screenwriter puts his own "spin" on the narrative. When interpreting a story, something fundamental is changed. It might be an attempt to make the story more acceptable to an audience. For example, many adaptations of William Shakespeare's plays, such as *West Side Story* (1961), are reinterpreted to play out in modern times. Interpretation does have its limits. It can raise some ethical dilemmas when dealing with so-called "true stories," because it becomes a misrepresentation of events that actually happened. Of course, no film will be completely accurate anyway, because film is fundamentally a kind of illusion.

Screenwriting is a very challenging endeavor, and it requires a lot of practice to refine the necessary skills. In the end, however, it is not the quality of the writing that will get a script produced, but the ability to market the story to those with enough power to make a production happen.

KEY POINTS:

- Most productions begin with the script or at least a story idea.
- The final script for a film will likely reflect the work of many individuals, but most will never receive credit.
- The Writers Guild of America has a detailed 27-page manual on how to determine screenwriting credits for everything but animated films.

- Producers are required to submit to the guild a list of proposed writing credits.

- Because the producers and directors have significant influence over the final film, they will not usually be given a writing credit.

- Animation writers are represented by The Animation Guild and not the WGA.

- If the story and the script are a product of the same writer(s), the credit will be "written by."

- If the story was written specifically for the film, the "story by" credit is used.

- If the screenplay is loosely based on another source the credit will read "screen story by."

- Rarely, the "adapted by" credit is used when the script closely follows the original source material.

- If two writers work together on a screenplay, their names will be joined with an "&."

- If two writers work on different drafts of the script, their names will be joined with an "and."

- Story and screenplay credits cannot be shared by more than two people, but a writing team is considered a single author.

- Screenwriters must also work to sell their scripts with a synopsis, a story treatment, and a logline.
- A synopsis is a one-page summary written in narrative form.
- A treatment tells the story in narrative form scene by scene and is usually around 40 pages.
- A logline is a one-sentence teaser describing the story.
- Screenwriters might pitch their stories to producers, studio executives, agents, managers, investors, directors, actors, or anyone else who might have the power to get a film produced.
- Screenplays should not be regarded as a final product, but as a means to an end.
- Screenplays are typically 120 pages long and written in a three-act structure with major transition points coming at one quarter and three-quarters of the way through the story.
- This standard helps to keep the production on track and helps audiences appreciate the story.
- Screenplays should be concise.
- Screenwriters should let the visuals, and not the dialogue, tell the story.

- Adaptations require screenwriters to use elision, interpolation, and interpretation to create their script.
- Elision is a compression of events.
- Interpolation is an alteration of the original narrative.
- Interpretation is a more substantial rewrite of the story.

CHAPTER SEVEN

PRODUCTION DESIGN

Consider these three motion picture stills.

One takes place in the South Pacific in 1943 - *South Pacific* (1958), one takes place in Renaissance Rome - *The Agony and the Ecstasy* (1965), and the third takes place in ancient Egypt - *Cleopatra* (1963). It isn't difficult to tell which one is which, and yet all three scenes were designed by the same man, the great production designer, John DeCuir.

It is the production designer's job to visually fix the film's narrative to a specific time and place, and to ensure that the film has an appropriate and consistent style. While the look of a film stems from the director's vision, it is primarily the production designer's responsibility to bring that vision, and by extension, the aesthetics of the film, to fruition.

The word "aesthetics" comes from the Greek word for beauty. However, the meaning has evolved, and aesthetics refers more to a beauty of appropriateness than one of attractiveness. For example, a dreary setting, like that in *Joe Versus the Volcano* (1990), can be aesthetically appropriate for a film while still being "ugly."

Joe Versus the Volcano (1990)

Aesthetically appropriate designs fit their films, and can be beautiful, but do not have to be. It is, therefore, a production designer's responsibility to ensure that, through the efforts of the other members of the art department, the design of a film is aesthetically appropriate for the director's vision.

Production designers are often inspired by the work of visual artists and they must possess the skills of a visual artist themselves. For example, Benjamin Robert Haydon's painting, "Napoleon Bonaparte" was clearly the inspiration for a scene in *The Duellists* (1977).

Napoleon Bonaparte - Benjamin Robert Haydon

The Duellists (1977)

In the end, however, production design must be pragmatic and may be more akin to graphic design than art. Production design must meet the needs of the narrative. Sometimes, when a production designer has limited options, the script may need to be rewritten to suit the available sets, costumes, and other resources. Related to this is the fact that production designers' creative freedom is limited by the budget, forcing the design to be limited to what is feasible for the production. For example, when *Cat People* (1942) was forced to complete production in 18 days on a minuscule budget, the designers chose to utilize the sets built for the recently completed *Magnificent Ambersons* (1942). And when they didn't have the money to convincingly portray the titular monsters, and they cloaked them in shadow, creating significantly more tension than the shots called for by the script.

Magnificent Ambersons (1942)

Cat People (1942)

The earliest equivalents to modern production designers were referred to as "technical directors," and they acted more like project managers than designers. They would gather a group of carpenters and other professionals to construct a set, and make sure they did so efficiently. The technical directors were more concerned with pragmatic than artistic results.

This began to change at the end of the silent era. Beginning around 1930, the technical directors started being referred to as "art directors." Each studio would have a large number of art directors working under a supervising art director. The supervisor would assign an art director to each production. Sometimes directors and art directors would develop a close, regular working relationship. If successful, they would be paired again in hopes of repeating that success.

Some directors objected to the use of the term "director" in the art director's title. As design became a more significant element in film, directors thought caused confusion about who was responsible for the artistic vision. This led to some clashes between the two professions' guilds. The "Society of Motion Picture Art Directors" (now known as the "Art Directors Guild") was founded in 1937, and the "Screen Director's Guild" (now known as the "Directors Guild of America") was founded in 1938. With the rise of color films, the art director's contributions gained even more respect and soon the title of "art director" had been used so frequently that the conflict died down.

Chapter Seven – Production Design

The term "production designer" was first used instead of "art director" in the credits for *Gone with the Wind* (1939). The intention was to acknowledge the extraordinary work of William Cameron Menzies, whose vision helped the film maintain consistency despite having five different directors. In time, the term "production designer" would become more commonplace.

William Cameron Menzies

In addition to creating the overall look of the film, production designers have numerous other responsibilities. Most importantly, they supervise the set designers, set decorators, prop makers, carpenters, and costume and makeup artists. Production designers will also work closely with the lighting department, even though they are the responsibility of the director of photography or cinematographer.

Determining whether a scene will be shot on a set or on location is another concern for a production designer. In the earliest days of motion pictures almost everything was filmed on a set because equipment was less mobile and there was greater need to control for lighting and weather. As equipment became more portable, location shooting was frequently preferred. Today, that trend is reversing because scenes are often more easily created with computers. For example, there is a scene in *The Wolf of Wall Street* (2013) that takes place

The Wolf of Wall Street (2013)

in Venice, Italy. The bulk of the scene was shot on an interior set at J.C. Studios in Brooklyn, NY, and when a single exterior establishing shot was needed, it was shot there too. Rather than transport the cast and crew to Italy for a shot that lasted mere seconds, the actors were filmed in front of a green screen and the shot was composited with a computer-generated Venetian background.

When location shooting is desired, the production designer will oversee that too. Some locations can be used unaltered, but most will need to be modified to match the demands of the film. One famous example of this occurred during the filming of *Raiders of the Lost Ark* (1981). When filming a Cairo terrace scene, 350 television antennas had to be removed from local buildings to present a 1930s skyline.

Raiders of the Lost Ark (1981)

Production designers also oversee costuming, hairstyling, makeup, and prosthetics, to ensure that they mesh with the overall design. A costume's aesthetic can be based on many factors, including historic or technical accuracy (for example uniforms), what looks flattering (or unflattering, if that is the intent), and what matches the film's visual style. In large crowd scenes, the color and style of the background performers' costumes help to establish the film's setting.

Special effects, like other aspects of production design, are usually delegated to various professionals, but they're coordinated with the artistic vision of the production designer and director. Due to the proliferation of computer-generated images (CGI), a production designer's work is increasingly digital. This involves making sure fantastic elements are tonally consistent, that CGI mock-ups look like the real sets, props, or costumes for which they're meant to stand in, and that any other CGI elements are aesthetically fitting for the world of the film.

In the early thirties, the Disney animation studio began "storyboarding" their films. Drawing inspiration from comic books, they posted on a wall a series of hand-drawn images that served as a guide for their animated films. Soon the same process was being used for live-action films. Sometimes storyboards are only drawn for key shots or scenes, but on occasion, they will be drawn for nearly every shot in the movie. This can save an enormous amount of time and money in the long run because key decisions can be made before shooting begins, and everyone on the production team will be working toward a single vision. On the other hand, it can take away from the spontaneity, and unexpected shots that opportunistically present themselves. It can also minimize the artistic efforts of the editors because they are somewhat constrained to replicate the storyboards. Sometimes a production designer will draw the storyboards, but because it is a time-consuming process, a storyboard artist is usually hired to work in collaboration with the director, production designer, and cinematographer.

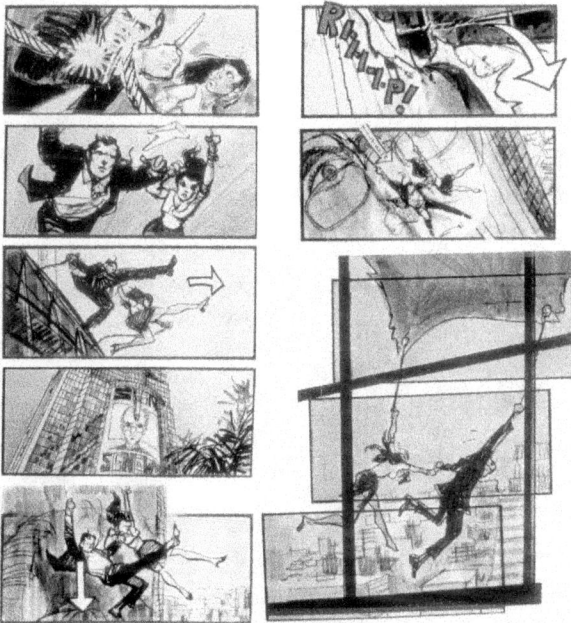

Storyboard for *Tomorrow Never Dies* (1997)

When done well, every visual element on the screen will have been placed there for a purpose and will contribute to the mise-en-scène - a French term meaning "placement in the scene." Sometimes the work of the production designer will be central to the film, as in the sweeping painterly look of *What Dreams May Come* (1998). Other times, the work of the production designer needs to remain softly blurred in the background so that it supports the action on screen without upstaging it, as in this scene from *Working Girl* (1988).

What Dreams May Come (1998)

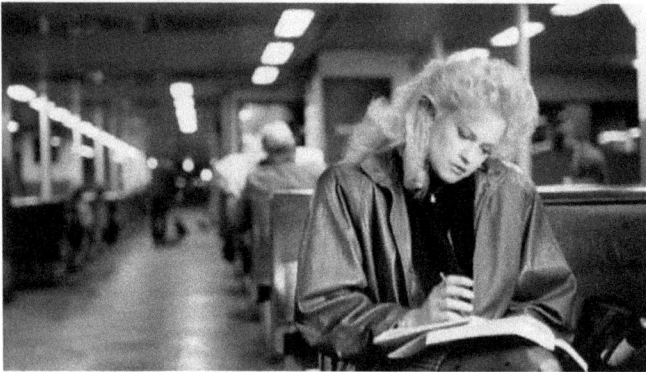

Working Girl (1988)

In any case, because film is a visual medium, the work of the production designer will always make a significant contribution to the narrative.

KEY POINTS:

- The production designer visually fixes a specific time and place to the film.
- The production designer must also create an appropriate and consistent style.
- Production designers rely on the work of visual artists for inspiration.
- Production designers must possess the skills of a visual artist.
- Production design must be pragmatic and meet the needs of the narrative.
- Practical constraints can lead to creative invention.
- Technical directors were production designers' predecessors, who largely served as project managers for the construction of sets.
- Later they were called "art directors" and were assigned to work on specific productions or certain directors.
- The director's guild clashed with the art director's guild over the use of the term, "director."
- In 1939, William Cameron Menzies was the first person to be credited as "production designer" for his work on *Gone with the Wind* (1939).
- Production designers supervise the set designers, set decorators, prop makers,

carpenters, costume and makeup artists, location scouts, and storyboard artists.

- The production designer is responsible for the look of each frame of film.
- In order to contribute to the narrative, the production designer must know when his efforts should take focus and when they should remain part of the background.

CHAPTER EIGHT

EDITING

Editors will tell you that films are assembled, not shot. Without a doubt, film footage is merely raw material until someone puts it in order. Some people dismissively suggest that editing is just a matter of subtraction; the objective is to simply cut out the bad scenes and leave the good ones.

There is, however, an art to removing the bad and leaving the good and the arrangement and timing of the good matters significantly. For example, imagine a simple conversation scene using two "over-the-shoulder" shots. The editor could bounce back and forth between the two shots in rapid-fire succession or abandon one entirely to focus on just one character. There isn't a right or wrong way to edit the scene, but there may be better or worse ways to deliver the desired message. It's a judgment call. This is where the art comes in.

Editing has been called the "silent art" because if it's done well, it won't call attention to itself. In truth, this is probably the case with all aspects of filmmaking. If a performance, or costume, or sound, or anything else asserts itself to the point where it distracts from the narrative, it's not fulfilling its artistic mission. A great narrative will have a seamless blend of all its elements.

However, it's the job of the editor to make that perfect blend happen.

The earliest films had no editing at all. Cameras were fixed in place and recorded the action that passed in front of them, and scenes simply continued until the camera ran out of film. The presumption was that audiences would find it weird or disconcerting if there were a sudden shift in time or place.

The earliest known film featuring more than one shot was Robert W. Paul's *Come Along, Do!* (1898). This British amusement had two scenes and ran about 60 seconds, but only the first 38 seconds have survived. The opening shows an old man and woman (presumably married) having lunch outside of an art museum. They finish their lunch and go into the museum. The following scene is lost (except for two single frames), but reportedly it shows the couple in the museum where the old woman becomes disgruntled that her husband is eyeing a nude statue. Theoretically, it's a comedy.

One could certainly argue that this doesn't rise to the level of art, but it was a major turning point for the art world. While there were certain instances in literature and live performance where scenes would shift to a new time or place, this is possibly the first instance of an edit for the purpose of maintaining continuity. The scene shifts seamlessly from the outside to the inside of the museum and the shift is made to further the narrative.

Come Along, Do! (1898)

Film editing would soon become routine, but before everyone caught on, a stage magician, Georges Méliès, used the weird disconcerting effect of editing to his advantage. Méliès would use in-camera edits (stopping and then later restarting the camera without changing the film, thereby causing a sudden change in the subject when the film was played) to create the illusion of appearances and disappearances on film. For example, in Georges Méliès' *The Haunted Castle* (1896), a magician makes a cauldron disappear through the clever use of an edit. Today that sort of illusion seems corny, but at the time, it astonished naïve audiences.

Some context is necessary to understand the importance that editing brings to narrative. Even the earliest works of literature would take leaps through space and time to tell their story. For example, Homer's *Iliad* is focused on a few weeks at the end of the Trojan War, but Homer makes references to prior events and even describes what will happen in future events. Nonetheless, the story is linear. In the novel, *The Life and Opinions of Tristram Shandy, Gentleman* (1759), the central joke is that Tristram is unable to tell his life story without taking many wild tangents, but again, the narrative progresses in a linear fashion. However, the first use of true parallel construction in narrative may have been in D. W. Griffith's film *The Sealed Room* (1909). In that film, a king finds his queen in the midst of a tryst with a court musician. Seeking revenge, he seals the lovers in a room where they run out of air and die. The action of the film moves back and forth between the room where the

The Haunted Castle (1896)

lovers are, and the adjacent room where the door is being bricked up. This quick but easy move back and forth between the contemporaneous scenes was truly groundbreaking and ushered in a new era of storytelling conventions.

The Sealed Room (1909)

Several months later Griffith made *A Corner in Wheat* (1909), a film that exploited this technique even further. The movie is the story of a (presumably) evil tycoon who corners the wheat market. The film bounces around back and forth to numerous locations including a farm, the tycoon's office, a general store, a trading pit, and a grain elevator. It's also worth noting that this is a silent film. Unlike literature, silent films had to relate their stories with pictures. Griffith used title cards in *A Corner in Wheat*, but not for dialogue. The title cards in that film served only as transitions to either establish a location (such as "A VISIT TO THE ELEVATORS") or for ironic commentary (such as "THE CHAFF OF THE WHEAT" before the scene of the poor lining up for bread at the general store). Remarkably, the film would be equally

A Corner in Wheat (1909)

effective without any title cards. Griffith lays out his narrative not just with pictures, but more importantly the juxtaposition of those pictures. Griffith was an indisputable master of storytelling through editing and he set the standard for all subsequent editors.

Early on, films were shot as though the audience were looking at a stage play. All the action was set behind a virtual "fourth wall," like the proscenium arch of a theater. In time (particularly as cameras became more mobile) filmmakers broke free of that fourth-wall convention. Cinematographers and editors then developed new conventions that are routinely understood by audiences today. The system which developed from this is broadly called "continuity editing."

Continuity editing begins with some sort of transition into a scene. This is usually a simple cut, a dissolve (where the previous scene fades out as the next one fades in), or a fade-in (where the scene fades in from a black screen). There are some less commonly used transitions such as a wipe, an iris in or out, or a push, but these types of transitions tend to call too much attention to themselves.

In continuity editing, the first shot of a scene is typically an establishing shot. This is a wide shot used to establish the overall area where the scene takes place. Sometimes an exterior shot will come first, and then a wide shot of the interior will follow. Once it is established where the scene takes place and what characters are in the scene, a series of shots and reverse shots will follow. The shots will alternate back and forth between characters pulling in closer and closer as the tension of the scene rises. Once the scene reaches its maximum tension (usually in a close-up) it will be followed by a medium shot of the characters again, and then back to a wide shot as the characters exit.

Here is an example from *The Young Philadelphians* (1959). Anthony Judson Lawrence (played by Paul Newman) and Joan Dickinson (played by Barbara Rush) have just met at a party. After dancing, the scene fades to their smoking cigarettes out on a patio. It begins with a wide shot to establish where they are. This is followed by a series of over-the-shoulder shots back and forth as they talk. When the conversation turns more serious, a series of close-up shots are used. Then, as the conversation wraps up, the characters stand, and the camera pulls back a bit for a two-shot. Finally, as the characters exit, the camera pulls back even further, and there is a fade to the next scene.

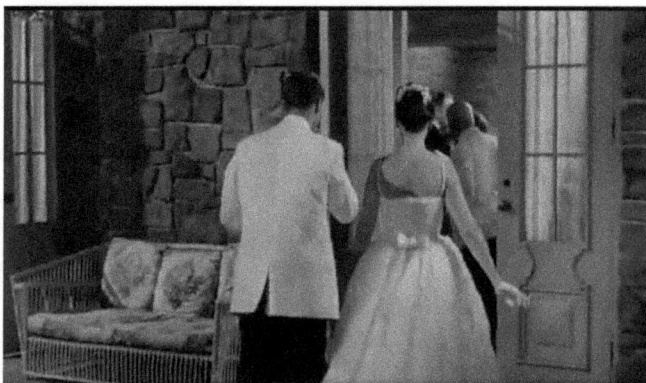

The Young Philadelphians (1959)

Of course, this is just the most conventional way of shooting a scene. It's quite useful because audiences are accustomed to it and it doesn't call attention to itself. However, there are no firm rules for editing, and mixing in a variety of shots (such as high or low camera angles, dolly, or tracking shots) can be very effective. The current trend is to resist conventional editing techniques unless a formal conventional feeling is desired. If that scene from *The Young Philadelphians* were being shot today, it would probably be done with a Steadicam moving around the actors and have no edits at all.

There are many other conventional shots that are used to preserve continuity. For example, a "match on action shot" continues the trajectory of a moving object from one shot to the next to create the illusion of continuous movement – even if the two shots were created hours, or even days apart.

For example, in the final scene of *McLintock!* (1963), G. W. McLintock (played by John Wayne) barges into the second-floor room of his wife, Katherine Gilhooley McLintock (played by Maureen O'Hara). McLintock then backs Katherine across the room until she is forced through some French doors and onto a balcony. The balcony rail then gives way, and she falls backward into a wagon full of hay. That sequence is made up of four distinct shots, but the action flows from one to the other seamlessly. However, it's worth noting that while the interior shots were filmed on a soundstage (on the ground floor no less), the exterior shots were filmed miles away on a backlot days later. Further, on closer inspection, it's easy to tell that the shot of her falling from the balcony was performed by a stunt **man** and not Maureen O'Hara. Nonetheless, when the shots are put together, the action appears seamless.

The illusion is accomplished in part because the sequence consistently moves from left to right on the screen. If the camera were moved to the other side of the room for one of the shots the action would move the other direction across the screen (right to left) and cause confusion for the viewer. Not only would the action not match, but it would break the 180° rule. The 180° rule is a convention that states that the camera must stay on one side of the action (i.e. not move more than 180° around the scene) unless a new establishing shot is used. The camera is effectively the eye of the audience; what the camera sees, the audience sees. If the camera is arbitrarily moved all over the scene the audience will feel like they were randomly jumping all over the scene too, and the continuity will be broken.

Another convention, however, allows the audience to momentarily break from the 180° rule and see the scene through the eyes of a character. Consider this example from *Dial M for Murder* (1954). Tony Wendice (played by Ray Milland) removes a photograph from the wall and shows it to Charles Swann (played by Anthony Dawson). The shot of Swann looking at the photo is followed by a shot of what he sees. (Note the famous cameo appearance of director, Alfred Hitchcock on the left.) The 180° rule is temporarily suspended as the audience gets a chance to look through the character's eyes.

The 30° rule is another editing convention. The camera angle must move more than 30° from one shot to the next, or it will look like a "jump cut." Just like the cauldron in Méliès' The Haunted Castle, there will be an apparent jarring shift in the visual that will call attention to itself.

The art and conventions of editing were studied in-depth at The Gerasimov Institute of Cinematography or VGIK (also known as The All Union Institute of Cinematography). The institute, founded in 1919, was the Soviet Union's national film school dedicated to the production of propaganda films. The school, now called The Russian State University of Cinematography, is the oldest film school in the world. Early Soviet filmmakers such as Sergei Eisenstein, Lev Kuleshov, Vladimir

Dial M for Murder (1954)

Gardin, and Dziga Vertov took editing beyond practical storytelling and used it for a thematic psychological effect. This developed into "montage theory."

"Montage" is a French word that means "mount" or "assemble." The Soviets used the term to refer to a style of editing in which the whole of a scene is greater than the sum of its parts. They theorized that the juxtaposition of shots could create a new meaning not represented in the

117

individual shots. For example, a shot of a smiling man is simply a shot of someone who is happy, but if that shot follows a shot of a girl in a bikini, the man will seem lecherous rather than happy. Not surprisingly, this theory was developed in the silent era, when it was necessary to tell the story through pictures.

The term "montage" can be confusing because over time it took on new meanings. It's sometimes simply used synonymously for the term "editing" (particularly in Europe), and it can also refer to an extended series of short shots (usually referred to as a "montage sequence").

Montage sequences have been used to accomplish many different effects. Typically, they will be used to speed up the narrative. This is helpful if a film wants to dispatch with a lot of exposition quickly or speed up the process of a hero going through some sort of training. In classic films, this would sometimes come in the form of a series of newspapers with dramatic headlines spinning toward the camera, or a series of town names to show a transcontinental journey. Montages have also been used for comic or sentimental effect showing a series of silly visuals or romantic moments. Montages can be used to compare or contrast as well, going back and forth between two characters or locations. Montages can also be used to slow down an otherwise frenetic film to add contrast or stretch time to add emphasis. For example, a murder scene that in reality would take an instant might be shown from multiple angles using multiple close-ups. Montages have been used for flashback or flash-forward sequences such as when a detective at the end of the story explains what really happened. Montages can also be surreal and be used for dream sequences or delusional experiences. Montages are usually supported by music or sound effects and have limited dialogue. On the other hand, some montages are purely auditory, as when a character is thinking or hearing voices in his or her head. For example, Alfred Hitchcock employed an auditory montage in *Psycho* (1960). When Marion Crane (played by Janet Leigh) is driving out of town with stolen money, she imagines what people will say when they find out what she's done.

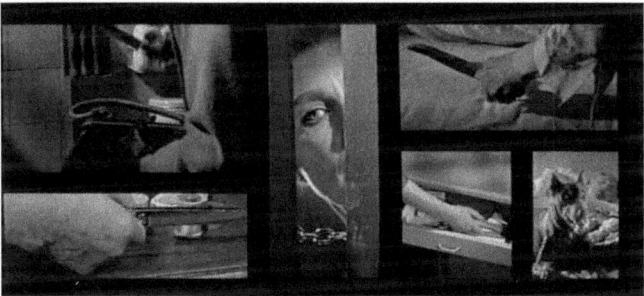

Boston Strangler (1968)

Split-screen is another editing technique that allows for the contemporaneous juxtaposition of images. While the technique dates back to the silent era, it reached its greatest popularity in the late 1960s and early 1970s with films like *The Thomas Crown Affair* (1968), *The Boston Strangler* (1968), and *Woodstock* (1970). The earliest uses of split-screen, such as showing two sides of a phone conversation, were very practical, but by the late

1960s, young filmmakers were using it for thematic and psychological effects. This was aligned with the rise of "pop culture," which focused in part on the mass inundation of multiple images. Filmmakers learned that viewers could take in information at a faster rate and having a split-screen was one way of accomplishing that. By the end of the 1970s however, the use of split screens was considered passé. Aided by better editing equipment, films in the 1980s began to use faster and faster cuts to deliver more images in a shorter time.

While the earliest editing was done in-camera by simply stopping and starting the film, by the 20th century, editing was accomplished with scissors and tape. At first, this was considered "women's work" (equivalent to

Women editing at the Empire Film Company

sewing) and was done almost exclusively by working-class women. Back then, the job was separated into two distinct positions (some women were "cutters" and others were "joiners") and the process was executed in a factory-like manner. Today, only 21% of editors are women.[3]

Moviola

Then, in 1924 a Dutch American filmmaker, Iwan Serrurier, invented the "moviola," a machine similar to a movie projector, but instead of projecting on a large screen, it projected on a small viewing screen for the operator. The film could be run backward or forward at varying speeds with the use of foot pedals, which allowed the operator to quickly find the precise place to cut the film. In the sound era, a second film strip containing the analog sound information would be run through simultaneously.

Sound and picture were recorded separately. This is why the iconic clapperboard (or slate) was used. On a major production, the second assistant camera operator would hold the clapperboard in front of the camera and announce what scene was about to be shot. In editing, the information written on the clapperboard would be matched with what the second assistant camera operator announces on the soundtrack. When the clapperboard is snapped closed it's easy to see on the film and hear on the soundtrack. This allows the sound and visual to be synched perfectly.

It would be easy to conclude that this made piecing a film together simple, but the process was often rushed and chaotic. Editors worked in low light among piles of notes and film cans, with strips of film festooned about the room. And when it was determined that a given piece was no longer needed, it literally ended up on the cutting room floor.

The next generation of editing machines were "flatbed" machines. Instead of running the film vertically, these machines ran the film horizontally across a large table. This allowed the editor to quickly synch multiple visual and audio tracks. The flatbed machines became popular in the early 1970s but were very slowly phased out in the late 1980s. Flatbed editors are still being manufactured, but mostly for film purists and preservationists.

Photo: DRs Kulturarvsprojekt

Steenbeck 16mm flatbed ST 921

"Non-destructive" editing came about slowly through the 1980s. It grew out of television video editing, where the use of videotape or laserdiscs were used to copy segments rather than splicing and destroying the original. This meant there were no longer piles of notes and lengths of film strewn about the floor. Unlike television, the film industry was slow to embrace video because of its inferior quality. However, filmmakers did like the immediacy of video. With the use of "video assist," they could record on location with video and film at the same time. This was good enough for immediate playback and editing in a non-destructive fashion. Once the editing decisions were made, the cuts would be marked on an "edit decision list," which would then be used to cut the actual film.

Ultimately, with the rise of superior digital filmmaking technology, all editing became digital, and the use of film stock became nearly obsolete. This allowed for computerized, "non-linear," editing in which all shots exist in a digital format. The technical information is automatically recorded, and the editor can quickly bounce back and forth between shots to make edits. This allows an editor the freedom to experiment and quickly save numerous versions of a scene.

The introduction of computers into the editing process allowed editors to make faster and faster cuts as the new millennium began. The average shot length in 1930 was eleven seconds, but the average shot length in 2006 was only four seconds. Some action films have an average length under two seconds, but this can be a little misleading. This is a "mean average," and doesn't reflect the "median" length of a shot. In a two-hour film, you can fit in more two-second shots than you can two-minute shots. Further, the length of a shot doesn't tell the whole story. A sixty-second shot filled with action can seem a lot more chaotic than fifteen four-second shots with no movement at all.[5]

In general, however, the use of computers has led to a postmodern, chaotic style of editing where the objective is not to move the narrative forward as much as it is to titillate the senses. Interestingly, as the edits have become more visually disorienting, filmmakers rely more heavily on sound to maintain continuity. A one-minute scene might have 20 visual cuts, but it's likely that the dialogue or music will be continuous and used to bind those visual cuts together into a comprehensible whole.

While fast editing is a staple of the action film, it can be controversial for the documentary filmmaker. Unedited, "raw" footage is considered more honest because it is seen through the "unblinking eye" of the camera. It can also be tedious to watch, leaving the documentarian in a difficult position.

The exact editing process will vary greatly from film to film. In general, the editor will begin work as the film is still being shot. Each day, clips (colloquially known as "dailies") are cataloged and reviewed by the editor for any problems or continuity issues. The editor will then begin to assemble a rough cut of each scene using a faster, low-resolution version, of the movie (or in the days of film, a "workprint"). This cut is not artfully done but serves as a jumping-off point. The producer and director will be coordinating with the editor through the whole process, but they will be more heavily involved as they work toward the so-called "first cut."

The director will be trying to maintain his artistic vision, and the producer will be looking to satisfy all legal and practical issues. It's the job of the editor to mediate between the director and producer and look for creative solutions that will satisfy both.

When most of the issues are resolved, a "fine cut" is made. This is where precise editing is employed, the color is corrected for consistency, and all the animation and optical effects are added. Then, for the "final cut," titles, sound effects, and music are added. At this point, there may be test screenings for audiences and if the feedback warrants it, additional scenes may be shot, and the film could be re-edited.

So, there is an initial cut created largely by the editor, a director's cut created with the director's involvement, and a final cut made under the producer's supervision. Producers are in charge of the final cut so they can double-check for legal issues like intellectual property infringement, be certain of the film's MPAA rating, and ensure that they fulfill any promises made to financers and distributors.

Sometimes, the editor will suggest the director reshoot a scene if a cut isn't working right. This happened more frequently before the days of video assist because the director couldn't always tell there was a problem until the film was developed and the editor began work. With digital technology, this sort of problem can be caught much sooner.

The art of editing continues to develop and change with society. Recent generations, who have grown up with the internet and gaming, tend to think in a nonlinear, "hyperlinked" manner. They're more tolerant of complex narratives and films that appeal to the senses more than the mind. This has led to an abundance of fast-paced visuals and an acceptance of jump cuts that break the $30°$ rule. The art of editing will continue to change as editors establish new conventions and find novel ways to break the rules.

KEY POINTS:

- Editing is the art of arranging the parts of a film to create a meaningful work of art.

- There are no right or wrong ways to edit, but there are better and worse ways to achieve the goal.

- Typically, good editing does not call attention to itself.

- The earliest experiments with film were quite short and did not use any editing.

- When editing was first employed, audiences found it jarring or magical.

- The concept of a non-linear narrative was not thoroughly explored prior to the development of film editing.

- Storytelling with editing relies as much on the juxtaposition of multiple images as it does on the content of the images themselves.

- It took many years to establish the film editing conventions that audiences now readily accept.

- Traditional editing involves a system called "continuity editing."

- In continuity editing, a scene begins with a transition into an establishing shot, followed by the camera slowly closing in on the action as tension rises. The camera then begins to pull back as the scene draws to a close.

- Contemporary films avoid traditional editing techniques preferring unusual angles or continuous Steadicam shots.

- Nonetheless, there are a variety of editing conventions that make the narrative easier to understand.

- Match on action shots, for example, continue the trajectory of a moving object from one shot to the next to create the illusion of continuous movement.

- The 180o rule is a convention that states that the camera must stay on one side of the action.

- The 180o rule will sometimes be temporarily suspended for a point of view shot.

- The conventions of editing (montage theory) were developed at The Gerasimov Institute of Cinematography.

- "Montage" is a French word that means "mount" or "assemble."

- A montage sequence is an extended series of short shots.

- Montage sequences can be used to speed up a narrative, for comic or sentimental effect, to compare or contrast things, to slow down a frenetic film, to stretch time for emphasis, to create flashbacks or flash-forwards, or to produce a surreal effect.

- Editors can use audio montages for the same purposes.

- A split-screen is another way to display multiple images at once.
- In the early days, editing was done by working-class women in a factory-like fashion.
- Today, only 21% of editors are women.
- Invented in 1924, the moviola was a machine that enabled editors to quickly make better artistic choices.
- Just the same, editors had to work in chaotic low light conditions.
- When a piece of film was no longer needed, it ended up on the cutting room floor.
- Flatbed editing machines, which became popular in the 1970s, allowed editors to work with multiple shots at once.
- "Non-destructive" editing, which was accomplished with video, came about in the 1980s.
- Computerized, "non-linear" editing became popular in the 21st century when motion pictures began to be shot on video.
- The average shot length today is less than half of what it was in the 1930s, but that isn't the only factor in creates the pace of a film.
- Editors will use sound to help create continuity in fast-paced scenes.
- Documentarians often prefer less editing to support the notion of the unblinking camera.

- The editing process begins with a rough cut that will be continually refined until the final cut is reproduced for distribution.
- The art of editing will continue to change as editors establish new conventions and find novel ways to break the rules.

CHAPTER NINE

MUSIC

Music was a major part of live theatre dating back to the ancient Greeks. Obviously, it was a major part of opera, musical theatre, and vaudeville too. By the end of the 19th-century melodramas (plays with incidental music) were popular, so it isn't surprising that film embraced music from the beginning as well. Thomas Edison was particularly keen to supply phonograph albums to accompany his silent films because he was a major player in the sound recording business as well.

By the turn of the twentieth century, phonographs had become common and inexpensive. Recording quality wasn't sufficient to convey the subtleties of an opera or symphony, but "tin pan alley" tunes were quite popular. Early film exhibitors, competing for entertainment dollars and looking to embrace the trend, sought ways of using music to accompany their films.

However, there was no standard approach to musical accompaniment early on. A 1909 article in *The Evening World*, describes the New York movie scene, and says a "Bowery artist with an accordion" provided accompaniment throughout the evening at one theater and passed his hat to make his wages.[6] While accordion accompaniment was atypical, it is certainly true that the experience varied from cinema to cinema. Most venues employed pianists or organists. However, some of the largest theaters had full-sized orchestras to accompany films.

The 1910's saw the introduction of feature length films, and the practice of musical accompaniment grew with it. "Photoplay" albums, which were a collection of pre-existing genre or mood music, were published specifically for the purpose of film accompaniment. The quintessential example of a photoplay album is Ernö Rapée's *Motion Picture Moods for Pianists and Organists, a Rapid Reference Collection of Selected Pieces, Adapted to Fifty-Two moods and Situations* (1924). This book contained a large collection of tabbed sheet music that allowed an accompanist to quickly turn to from one theme to the next. Often the accompanist would bluff their way through the first showing of a film because they hadn't seen it, but by the end of the run, the accompaniment was perfected. Eventually, cue sheets were published in trade magazines, and before long, the studios themselves began issuing cue sheets tailored to individual films, and eventually big-budget films had completely synchronized scores for their presentation in cinemas.

Composer Joseph Carl Breil penned the first fully synchronized score for a short film, *Queen Elizabeth* (1912) as well as the first fully synchronized score for a feature film, D. W. Griffith's *The Birth of a Nation* (1915). For that film, he created an extraordinary Wagnerian-style score using leitmotifs. In fact, the love theme for that film, the appropriately titled "*The Perfect Song*," became the first popular song written for a film. Nonetheless, the studios were resistant to musical scores, viewing them as an unnecessary expense.

The Jazz Singer (1927) is famous for being the first feature-length motion picture with not only a synchronized recorded music score, but also lip-synchronous singing and speech in several isolated sequences. For the most part the film is silent and uses title cards, however, its release presaged the introduction of the sound era and the implementation of the recorded musical score.

Eugenie Besserer and Al Jolson in *The Jazz Singer* (1927)

While earlier films employed classical and popular music themes, Max Steiner, considered the father of film music, wrote the first entirely original recorded musical score for *King Kong* (1933). As usual, the studio (RKO) was skeptical about spending a lot of money on the score. Nonetheless, Steiner was able to persuade them. The studio was afraid the film's special effects weren't working, and Steiner convinced them the music could help improve the film's pace. By closely associating the music to narrative events, the concept of the classical Hollywood score was born and Steiner went on to score more than three hundred feature films.

Max Steiner

In the late 1930s and through the 40s Hollywood made many musicals. However, even in dramas, it was almost obligatory to have a nightclub scene, with popular musicians performing a number. Hollywood learned that music associated with a film could be sold as sheet music, piano rolls, or recordings, to create an incremental revenue stream, and using big-name musical talent such as Bing Crosby, Carmen Miranda, or Benny Goodman, was a great way to garner publicity. In the late 1940s and early 1950s, singing cowboys like Roy Rogers, Tex Ritter, and Gene Autrey became popular.

Barbara Stanwyck singing "Drum Boogie" with Gene Krupa and His Orchestra in *Ball of Fire* (1941)

The first soundtrack to be released as an album was arguably that of Walt Disney's *Snow White and the Seven Dwarfs* (1938), but many more would follow. Throughout the 1950s and 60s Broadway musicals like *Oklahoma!* (1955) and *The Sound of Music* (1965) found their way to film, and jazz soundtracks like those from *Some Like It Hot* (1959), *Anatomy of a Murder* (1959), and *Á Bout de Souffle* (1960) were popular as well.

Featuring "Rock Around the Clock" by Bill Haley and the Comets, the first film to use a rock and roll song was *Blackboard Jungle* (1955). The song had been released the previous year but gained little attention until it was used in the movie. The film employs the song as an anthem for delinquent youth, and it's likely the film's popularity contributed to the idea that rock and roll would corrupt society.

The 1960s saw the movies fully embrace rock and roll, though it was sometimes unclear whether the albums were a byproduct of the movies, or the movies merely existed to market the albums. Elvis Presley, The Beatles, Chubby Checker, Herman's Hermits, The Monkees, and many others had films that were not nearly as good as the music featured in them.

Ann-Margret and Elvis Presley in *Viva Las Vegas* (1964)

By the end of the 1960s, it became cheaper and easier to make films, giving rise to an independent film movement. Just the same, a musical score was often a luxury for independent filmmakers until the era of digital music. Today, time, talent, and imagination are greater limiting factors than money for musical scores.

Film music is completely embraced as an artistic convention by audiences now. It never strikes an audience as odd that orchestral music, might be accompanying a character hiking alone in the wilderness. Of course, musical scores had long been found in opera, dance, and musical theatre, but music is the focus of those arts. Film pioneered the concept of non-diegetic music (music without an apparent source within the world of the story) supporting the narrative.

Film music can serve many different purposes. The chief purpose is to set the tone of the film by clueing the audience into the genre or intensity of the film. It can alert the audience to the emotions of a specific character or signal the significance of a specific moment. Music has a psychological impact on an audience too. It can create an urgency or a disquieting effect, or it can lull an audience into a state of complacency. In the same way, music can be used to trick the audience. It can bolster a propaganda film with a sense of patriotism, or it can intentionally mislead an audience in a whodunit or horror film.

Music can establish time and place in a film. For example, sitar music or an Irish jig will certainly establish geography, as would certain familiar tunes like, "Rule, Britannia!" Music can also take audiences to fictional worlds and even into dreams or nightmares by using unusual or disconcerting music. Harpsichord music will set a film in the 18th century, and big band music will place it in the 1940s. Period music can also be used to help signify a flashback scene.

Film music will also be in accord with the intimacy (or lack of intimacy) in a scene. A romantic scene in a small room will employ a minimum of instruments playing in a high register, while an action scene might employ a full orchestra, making greater use of a lower register. By moving back and forth between the two, a contrast can be created that could be instructive to the narrative.

Finally, one of the most important and often subtle psychological effects of music is to create audience cohesion. There can be no doubt that watching a film at home is a very different experience from seeing it in a crowded theater. Even though audience members might enter a theater with differing moods or preconceived ideas about a film, herd behavior, guided by musical stimulus, will begin to affect the mood of the entire audience, and their perception of the film.

In the early days of film, musical cues were never subtle. The overuse of leitmotifs and grandiose tunes were often emotional redundancies. In fact, the word "melodrama" literally means, "musical drama," and the abuse of it is what gives the word its negative connotation.

Mickey Mouse's first film, *Steamboat Willie* (1928), famously features the iconic mouse in a pantomime working on a steamboat. In the film, every

139

gesture and movement is timed perfectly to the musical score. This has a marvelous comedic effect that's perfectly suited to that film, but the effect would be silly in just about anything other than a cartoon. Ever since, when composers tie a score too closely to the action on the screen, it is pejoratively referred to as "Mickey Mousing." An example of how this can be used effectively outside of a cartoon is the famous comedic sword fight in *The Princess Bride* (1987), where the beats of the music match the strokes of the battle.

The Princess Bride (1987)

Alternatively, the score will sometimes come first, and the action will be edited to match it. This often occurs in small-budget films that cannot afford an original score. However, these films are usually not edited so closely to the music that it results in Mickey Mousing.

In 1995 two Danish directors started a film movement called "Dogme 95," which sought to "purify" the filmmaking process by creating a vow of poverty. Among other things, the vow stated that music must not be used unless it occurs within the scene being shot. By only using diegetic sound (that which can be sourced to the world portrayed in the film) Dogme 95 adherents shun musical scores and the cost that comes with them. While the Dogme 95 movement found some truth in eliminating as much artifice as possible, the movement didn't last long because the art of film ultimately relies on artifice.

The process of scoring a film has changed little over the years, except for the influence of new technology. A composer might begin work early in the process to engage with other designers, or if the music is integral to specific scenes (as with a musical). More often, however, the composer will begin work during postproduction when the editing begins in earnest.

Sometimes a temporary soundtrack will be used to help the director, editor, and composer establish the style and tempo that will be used in the final film. This temporary score will be taken from already published pieces with a quality that the director believes will fit specific scenes. However, sometimes the director will see the film edited to the temporary score and not be able to imagine other music in its place. Famously, director, Stanley Kubrick and editor, Ray Lovejoy used Richard Strauss' tone poem "Also sprach Zarathustra" and Johann Strauss II's "An der schönen blauen Donau" among other pieces for a temporary score while editing *2001, A Space Odyssey* (1968). The intention was to replace the music with a score written by composer Alex North, but ultimately Kubrick concluded that the temporary track was superior and used it in the final film. North attended the film's premiere not knowing that his score was discarded, and his name removed from the credits.

Typically, the scoring process will begin with spotting sessions. Spotting occurs after the director and editor have locked down the film, meaning that no further visual edits can be made. This is critical. The addition or subtraction of just a few frames will only alter the timing by a fraction of a second, but those fractions can quickly add up and throw the sound off completely. The spotting session will always be attended by the editor, director, and composer, but sound editors and producers will frequently attend as well. They will go through the film looking for (spotting) moments when the music will change in some way. As they go, the sound editor will document the precise timing and duration of the music as well as any comments that are made.

Each frame of the film will be marked with a SMPTE time code. This is a standard developed by the Society of Motion Picture and Television Engineers – thus SMPTE. The time code is in hours, minutes, seconds, and frames. Typically, a film will run at 24 frames per second, so a time code that reads 01:08:59:14 would be at one hour, eight minutes, fifty-nine seconds, and fourteen frames.

Music is a subjective thing, so collaboration can be challenging. A musical score is like an unseen actor. Because the score can add depth or counterpoint to the action on the screen, a director must coach a composer just as they would an actor. Even if a temporary score has been used, the composer and director must agree on how the final score will be differentiated from the temporary one. For this reason, directors usually like to work with composers with whom they have a close working relationship.

Sometimes the composer will get a chance to see the film before the spotting session and be able to play some ideas for the director at that time. However, it's not practical to compose while a director is looking over your shoulder. Musical composition is a very solitary practice at times, and directors and producers can be a little more than nervous when they send a composer off to work by themselves. The composition for a feature film can take as little as six weeks. The composer will usually meet with the director to share ideas during the process, but sometimes they won't meet again until the composition is complete.

With the use of computers and SMPTE codes, a film score can be created with precision. For example, imagine an action scene that lasts a minute and a half. Within that scene there may be a dozen "hit points" that the composer wishes to emphasize – perhaps a car crashes, a punch is thrown, a door is kicked in, etc. The composer will flag these moments using a software program and then rank them by importance. The computer will then suggest a selection of time signatures and tempos that will allow the composer to maximize the number of hit points that will be on the beat. Ideally the beats of the music will be within two or three frames ($1/12^{th}$ to $1/8^{th}$ of a second) of a hit point. This sounds a little extreme, but if the 12 hit points were each off by an $1/8^{th}$ of a second in the same direction, the scene would be off by 1.5 seconds by the end. Once the best tempo is selected, the computer will create a "click track," (a metronomic beat) that will keep the composer's timing perfect. Remarkably, before the digital age, a composer would have to work all of that out with pen and paper.

When the final score is approved, it will then be arranged. Sometimes the orchestration will be done by the composer, but more frequently time won't permit that. Consequently, some composers will have a preferred partner who does the arrangement for them.

The music supervisor will then organize a recording session in a studio where the film can be played as the music is being recorded. Sometimes the composer will conduct, but not always. Obviously, the size of the studio will depend on the number of musicians required. The conductor and musicians wear headsets so they can hear the click track as the recording is in process.

The music editor will also add temporary vertical lines, called "streamers," to the film frame. These lines are a timing device. They move across the screen from left to right to warn the conductor that a hit point is coming.

When the streamer reaches the right side of the screen it will be followed by a "punch," a small flash to signal the hit point.

Howard Shore conducting the recording of
The Hobbit: An Unexpected Journey (2012)

Smaller budget film and video will use MIDI (Musical Instrument Digital Interface) synthesizers and sequencers to replicate the sound of acoustic musical instruments. This is far less expensive than hiring an orchestra or even a small band. It has the added bonus of giving the composer complete control of the finished score and the ability to easily alter the recorded sound. According to a government study done by the National Center for Biotechnology Information only 68.6% of average music consumers could distinguish sampled music from acoustic recordings when played consecutively and only 72.5% of experts could distinguish the performances.[7] While the difference remains significant, the cost-saving, coupled with improving technology and consumer acceptance of electronically generated music, means there will certainly be more of it used in the future.

In the end, film composers get very little respect from their peers in the broader music industry. Even film composer John Williams, who has become household name and has proven his talent beyond screen music, is dismissed by those in the classical music world. Film scores are not considered pure art. They are pragmatic. They don't exist for their own sake, but rather they exist in support of a film. To a purist, that makes them something less than art, but to general audiences, they are the music of our times.

KEY POINTS:

- Music has been a part of entertainment for millennia and has been associated with film from the early years of the medium.
- Early on, Thomas Edison produced phonograph records to accompany his silent films.
- "Tin pan alley" tunes were more popular in early days of recording than operas or symphonies because of quality issues, and early film exhibitors embraced the trend.
- Initially cinemas employed pianists or organists to accompany silent films, but

some large theaters had full-sized orchestras.

- Collections of pre-existing genre or mood music called "Photoplay" albums were published for film accompaniment.

- Then cue sheets were published in trade magazines cinema accompanists.

- The studios eventually began issuing official cue sheets.

- Only big-budget films had completely synchronized scores.

- Composer Joseph Carl Breil penned the first fully synchronized score for a feature film, D. W. Griffith's *The Birth of a Nation* (1915).

- "*The Perfect Song*," became the first popular song written for a film.

- Studios often viewed musical scores as an unnecessary expense.

- *The Jazz Singer* (1927) is the first feature-length film with lip-synchronous singing and speech in several isolated sequences.

- The father of film music, Max Steiner, wrote the first entirely original recorded musical score for *King Kong* (1933).

- Steiner went on to score more than three hundred feature films.

- During the golden age of Hollywood, it was routine to have a popular musician perform in a nightclub scene and in the 1950s singing cowboys became popular too.

- Incremental income could be made by selling sheet music, piano rolls, or recordings of movie music.
- The first soundtrack to be released as an album was from *Snow White and the Seven Dwarfs* (1938).
- Broadway musicals and films with a jazz soundtrack became popular in the 1950s and 60s.
- *Blackboard Jungle* (1955) was the first film to use a rock and roll song, and likely created the idea that rock music could corrupt society.
- Film pioneered the concept of non-diegetic music (music without an apparent source) and it is now embraced as a common convention.
- Music can establish the genre or intensity of the film, create a mood, or signal the significance of a specific moment.
- Music can establish time and place in a film.
- Music can also foster audience cohesion.
- The over-use of leitmotifs and grandiose tunes in the early days of film were literally "melodramatic," and gives the word its negative connotation.

- Tailoring a musical score too closely to the action is pejoratively called "Mickey Mousing."
- Small-budget movies will sometimes edit the film to the established music instead creating a score to match the action.
- Some filmmakers avoid non-diegetic music for the sake of "reality."
- Composers will usually begin work during postproduction.
- To aid editing, a temporary soundtrack is sometimes used to establish the style and tempo.
- The scoring process begins with "spotting sessions" to find moments when the music will shift.
- Society of Motion Picture and Television Engineers (or SMPTE) time codes allow the music to be synced to a specific frame of film.
- While a composer must coordinate the director and design team, musical composition is usually a solitary practice.
- Computers are extremely valuable in helping create a score that is perfectly timed to the "hit points" (key moments of action) in the film.
- A "click track," (a metronomic beat) will be created to keep the musician's timing perfect when recording.

149

- Sometimes the orchestrations will be done by the composer, but more frequently it will be arranged by someone else.
- The music supervisor will organize a recording session in a studio where the film can be played as the music is being recorded.
- The conductor and musicians wear headsets so they can hear the click track as the recording is in process.
- The music editor will also add traveling vertical lines, called "streamers," and flashes called "punches" to the projected film to help time hit points.
- Small budget productions will use MIDI (Musical Instrument Digital Interface) synthesizers and sequencers to replicate the sound of acoustic musical instruments.
- Film composers get very little respect from their peers in the music industry because film scores are considered more pragmatic than artistic.

CHAPTER TEN

DOCUMENTARY FILMMAKING

Robert J. Flaherty's classic examination of the day-to-day life of an Inuit hunter and his family in the Canadian wilderness, *Nanook of the North* (1922), is known for establishing the principles of documentary filmmaking. However, in time, Nanook drew criticism because of its inaccuracies and the fact that many scenes were staged. For example, the Inuit were shown hunting with spears when they typically hunted with guns. A fake igloo was constructed to more easily film staged interior

Nanook of the North (1922)

shots, and the subject of the film, Nanook, wasn't really named Nanook. The film's defenders point out that the concept of documentary hadn't been fully codified in 1922, and many of the staged elements were necessary because of technical limitations. Given that, is Nanook a documentary? What is a documentary?

A documentary is a nonfiction film that's grounded in accuracy. However, there is often a lot of gray area when trying to present facts, truth, and reality. Some narrative films have strong thematic and storytelling connections to real events, but nonetheless, they wouldn't be regarded as documentaries. Consider the film, *Lenny* (1974), a biopic about the influential but arguably obscene comic, Lenny Bruce. Even though it was a big-budget feature film starring Dustin Hoffman and Valerie Perrine, it was made to look like a low-budget documentary from the 1960s. The film was shot in black and white, and included faux interviews with people from Bruce's life interspersed with what looked like vintage footage of Lenny Bruce.

Narrative films might fictionalize real events, but documentaries seek to record them. Just the same, documentaries are almost always biased in some fashion. Every filmmaker has opinions and must pick and choose what they put in their film, so even the most even-handed documentary will have a slight bias.

The very earliest motion pictures were documentaries. In 1878, photographer, Eadweard Muybridge, famously used a series of cameras to

Honey Bruce (played by Valerie Perrine) records an
interview for a "documentarian" in *Lenny* (1974).

determine whether horses take all four hooves off the
ground while running. The resulting series of pictures
presages the documentative utility of film. In fact, most
of the earliest films were simple experiments, recording
events like workers leaving a factory, a train departing a
station, or sporting events. These films, known as
"actualities," were entirely observational, and did not bear
any significant influence by the filmmaker.

There are three ways to classify documentaries:
by their purpose, by their content, and by their method of
creation. Documentaries have two main purposes, to
inform and to persuade. Informative documentaries are
educational in nature. While not always successful,
informative documentaries usually attempt to mitigate
their bias. *March of the Penguins* (2005), for example, is
simply about the lives of emperor penguins in Antarctica.
Persuasive documentaries, on the other hand, embrace

their bias. They make no pretense of objectivity. Unlike informative documentaries, a persuasive documentary will rely heavily on pathos. For example, in *Sicko* (2007), filmmaker Michael Moore skewers the American health care system while championing the systems in other nations.

Another way to classify documentaries is by their content. American documentary theorist Bill Nichols cites six major documentary "modes": poetic, rhetorical, observational, participatory, reflexive, and performative.[8] These modes are not mutually exclusive, and a documentary might use them consecutively or concurrently.

Poetic documentaries are films which have no pre-determined structure. They have no clear narrative and their intended purpose is to simply make an emotional appeal. Some sources, such as the Library of Congress, consider poetic documentaries a subset of experimental films, a category distinct from documentaries. For example, the film *Baraka* (1992) simply shows beautiful, expertly recorded scenes of daily life from around the world without any words or narrative structure.

An expository documentary is a rhetorical construct. It will often rely on a narrator or other prominent voice, explaining a position or message to the audience. Images are of secondary concern in this sort of documentary, and they attempt to present an air of objectivity and authority. For example, the first of seven films in the "Why We Fight" series produced by the

United States War Department, *Prelude to War* (1942), features a narrator explaining why it was necessary for the US to participate in World War II.

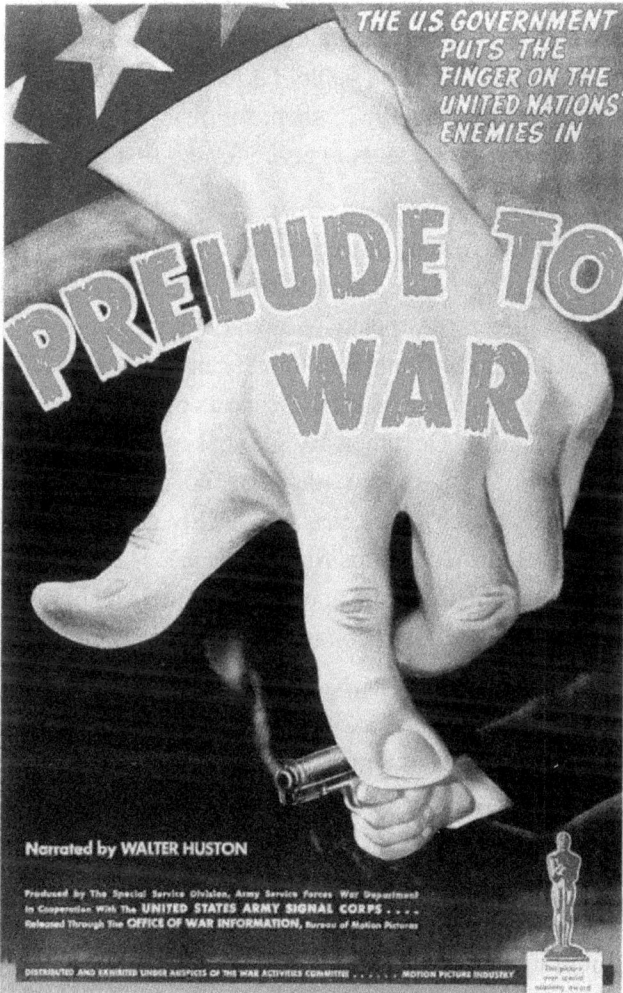

Prelude to War (1942)

Observational documentaries endeavor to present reality. They capture their subjects with as little planning or intervention as possible. Observational documentaries became popular in the 1960s with the advent of lightweight portable film equipment that made their fly-on-the-wall approach possible. *Le Joli Mai* (1963) shows life in Paris in May 1962, when, following the ceasefire with Algeria, France was at peace for the first time in 23 years.

Participatory documentaries take the opposite approach. Their assumption is that capturing something on film affects the behavior of the film's subject. To mitigate this, the filmmaker directly involves himself in the action, establishing his presence as part of the reality of the situation. Documentary filmmaker Ross McElwee set out one summer to make a film about General Sherman's march to the sea, but quickly got bored with the idea. So instead, in his film *Sherman's March* (1985), he decides to make a film about his own melancholy, love life, and lack of motivation to make the film.

The reflexive documentary takes the participatory approach even further. It attempts to affirm the artifice of the film, by calling attention to the fact that it is a constructed work of art and not a window into reality. It seeks to dispel the hypnotic allure of the cinema. The filmmaking process itself is usually the central concern of a reflexive documentary. For example, Nick Broomfield's *Driving Me Crazy* (1988) started out as a behind-the-scenes look at the mounting of Andre Heller's stage musical, *Body and Soul* in Berlin. In the end, it became a behind-the-scenes look at the challenges of documenting that effort. In this scene, lighting designer Michael Lesser, argues with film director Nick Broomfield about getting the film lights mounted before rehearsals begin.

Driving Me Crazy (1988)

Performative documentaries are more personal. The filmmaker himself is often the central subject of the film. Performative documentaries focus on the filmmaker's experience and emotions. They show the audience the filmmaker's point of view. In doing so, the filmmaker breaks the fourth wall and attempts to create a direct relationship with the audience. This mode of documentary often investigates the experience of a subculture. When feature film director Tom Shadyac recovered from a nearly fatal cycling accident, he began asking himself some fundamental questions. In his performative documentary, *I Am* (2010), he speaks with intellectual and spiritual leaders about what's wrong with our world and how we can improve it.

The third way to classify documentaries is by how they're made. There are three broad trends, which can mix and overlap to create a specific documentary's individual style.

A formal documentary tends to be structured and polished. It involves a fully equipped crew, formal interviews, and is often created for publicity. However, a formal documentary can also be an exposé, an investigation, or an outsider's attempt to gain perspective on the subject. They are planned in advance, have comparatively higher budgets than other types of documentaries, and are usually done in cooperation with an organization. This organization is not necessarily the subject of the documentary. It could simply be a like-minded group who supports the making of the film or even a branded documentary. For example, *Worn Wear: a Film About the Stories We Wear* (2013), produced by the Patagonia clothing company, highlights the stories of colorful customers who cherish their well-worn clothing.

The informal documentary is characterized by a low budget, minimal planning, and on-the-fly camerawork. In some cases, it is meant to create a "cinema verité" (French for true cinema) effect by capturing the subject without any artifice. Other times, this style is a result of the filmmaker's lack of funds or the necessity to film surreptitiously. For example, *The Cove* (2009) has relatively high production values, but the filmmakers were forced to capture much of their footage in secret as part of an exposé of the dolphin fishing industry.

A night vision scene from *The Cove* (2009)

Finally, the subject matter of some documentaries cannot be filmed. This includes things like historic occasions (because it is too late to capture them), concepts that can be described but not seen, or things that are too small, too large, too dangerous, or too distant to properly capture. In these instances, the documentarian can't rely on showing the audience what actually occurs. Instead, they must rely on images, recreations, interviews with experts, and / or narration. For example, when Werner Herzog set out to explore the world's most dangerous active volcanoes for his film, *Into the Inferno* (2016), he ironically had to do it at a safe distance.

Werner Herzog in *Into the Inferno* (2016)

These are not the only ways to create a documentary, and there is a great deal of overlap between them. For example, a historical documentary may use formal documentary techniques to interview people who remember a past event, and a cinema verité style to capture the surrounding area as it now exists.

Documentaries also have technical concerns. Fiction filmmaking can and often does occur in a completely controlled environment. A documentarian, on the other hand, must work with the world as it exists in front of the camera lens. Many documentaries have been dragged down by inarticulate interviewees or passing motorcycles.

However, even a properly conducted interview can become visually uninteresting rather quickly because there is little movement. This is where B-roll, an essential part of any documentary, comes into play. B-roll is "filler" footage taken for a documentary that can illustrate a point, be placed over an interview to disguise edits, or provide motion.

Documentary film equipment can present its own challenge. Because documentarians need to go to where the story is, it's sometimes necessary to transport heavy equipment very quickly, and fit it into small spaces. Further, some film equipment can be too expensive for a small-budget documentary, especially if it is being used in a hazardous situation. Documentarians are frequently forced to use smaller, or cheaper equipment that has a noticeably lower technical quality, relative to that used in narrative or experimental films. However, technology is constantly improving. Entire documentaries have been shot on a phone camera. And tiny so-called "action cameras," such as the "GoPro," are now being taken underwater or even aloft on miniature drones, and they can be mounted on robots or on all kinds of helmets or sporting equipment.

Using a camera or microphone skillfully takes practice, and documentarians don't always have second chances. Thus, a documentary filmmaker must be intimately familiar with the use of their equipment in order to record things right the first time.

Sound is usually the most challenging technical aspect of documentary filmmaking. Narrative films have the advantage of being able to plan, and the luxury of using sophisticated equipment. The documentarian, on the other hand, frequently needs to improvise and is often forced to film in areas not conducive to recording sound. Documentarians must be mindful of ambient sound and will sometimes resort to subtitles or dubbing if an interviewee's voice is indiscernible.

Documentarians also have an ethical and legal obligation to be mindful of what they include or exclude in their film. Libel is a major concern. While a filmmaker might not intend to commit libel, someone who is being filmed might say something that could get the filmmaker sued. To avoid this, interviews may need to be edited, or disclaimers added.

Most importantly documentaries should not be thought of as a single genre of film. Like narrative films, the category of documentaries is far too broad and varied in subject matter and style to fit any traditional definition of "genre." As noted in this chapter, documentaries can be informative, persuasive, poetic, expository, observational, participatory, reflexive, performative, formal, informal, representative, or a combination of those things.

So, is *Nanook of the North* a documentary? While some of the film was inaccurate and staged, it is earnest in its attempt to portray the Inuit as they once lived. The most significant contribution of the film though was to combine the observational qualities of actualities, with a narrative structure. This was something that had never been done before. It turns out that the mere unblinking eye of a camera is not necessarily the best way to document the truth. It is more effective to add context and grow to a point. Truth is something greater than mere accuracy. Yes, Nanook is a terrific documentary, and it blazed the trail for all subsequent documentaries.

KEY POINTS:

- A documentary is a nonfiction film that's grounded in accuracy.
- However, there is often a lot of gray area when trying to present facts, truth, and reality.
- Documentaries are almost always biased in some fashion.
- Documentaries are the oldest form of film.
- Some documentaries are intended to provide information to their audience.
- Others are meant to convince their audience of a position.
- A common way of breaking down documentaries splits them into six modes.

- Poetic documentaries overlap with experimental films and are an artistic sequence of images.
- Expository documentaries communicate a message.
- Observational documentaries seek to present something as it is and without comment.
- Participatory documentaries rely on the idea that filming something fundamentally alters it, so it is more honest if the director is actively involved in the documentary.
- Reflexive documentaries avoid attempting to present reality and instead revel in their own artifice.
- Performative documentaries are a form of self-examination by a filmmaker.
- Documentaries can also be broken down into more flexible categories via stylistic and budget-related elements.
- Formal documentaries have high budgets, good production values, and heavily emphasize formal interviews and a coherent message.
- Informal documentaries are created quickly with light, cheap equipment, and hasty camerawork, either as an intentional stylistic choice or a matter of necessity.

Chapter Ten – Documentary Filmmaking

- The subject matter of some documentaries such as historic occasions, concepts, or things that are too small, too large, too dangerous, or too distant cannot be filmed.
- Documentary filmmakers frequently face technical problems.
- B-roll is "filler" footage taken for a documentary that can illustrate a point, be placed over an interview to disguise edits, or provide motion.
- Documentarians may need to use lower quality equipment than narrative filmmakers, but technology is constantly improving.
- Recording sound can be especially difficult in documentary filmmaking.
- Documentaries must be especially careful to avoid libel and intellectual property infringement.
- Documentary is not a single film genre because there are many types of documentaries.
- Documenting the truth requires more than the unblinking eye of the camera; it is necessary to add context and grow to a point.

CHAPTER ELEVEN

TECHNOLOGY

Film is an extraordinary art form because it requires technology to both make it and to appreciate it. No other art form has this same restriction. (Radio, television, video games and the internet are generally regarded as media and not art forms, but feel free to quibble.) Most artistic disciplines date back to antiquity. People have been painting, sculpting and dancing since the beginning of time, but film simply wouldn't exist without late 19th / early 20th-century technology.

In fact, in the earliest years of film, the industry was more concerned with owning the rights to the technology than they were about the content of the films themselves. Film began not as a single invention but as a confluence of developments.

The industry traces its roots to simple toys that demonstrate the principle of persistence of vision - the phenomenon that when the human eye views a series of similar but changing images, they appear to be a single, moving image. There were many such toys in the 19th century including the thaumatrope, the kineograph (flipbook), the zoetrope, the phenakistoscope, the zoöpraxiscope, and many others. Combined with innovations in photography (including superior lenses and flexible photosensitive film) this was the foundation of the industry.

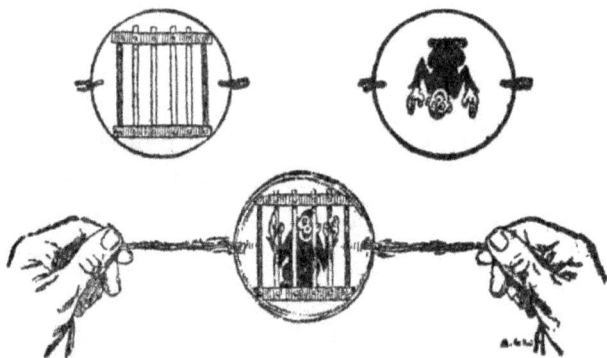

THE THAUMATROPE.

Above: How the designs of the two sides are placed with respect to each other.
Below: The combined image when the thaumatrope is twirled.

The first experiment with sequential photography (rather than drawn images) to exploit persistence of vision was conducted by Eadweard Muybridge, a British photographer. To satisfy an employer's wager as to whether horses take all four feet off the ground at once

while running, he devised an apparatus to capture every moment of a horse's travel across a track. He set up a long series of still cameras wired to strings that a horse would pull as it ran past. He was then able to use his invention, the zoöpraxiscope (a projector with a wheel of photographs) to show the images in rapid succession. This was the first photographic motion picture.

The Muybridge zoöpraxiscope

Muybridge's set-up required many cameras, but George Eastman, founder of the Eastman Kodak Company, made it possible to capture such moving pictures with a single camera. In 1880, Eastman patented the first practical perforated film rolls (initially on paper and then later on celluloid) that would allow a single camera to take numerous pictures without reloading.

Thomas Edison's Menlo Park "invention factory" made significant contributions to the introduction of film as well. It was a natural progression that Edison would want to capture moving pictures, having made a series of other inventions that recorded and repeated information, including the repeating telegraph and the phonograph. However, as a man who was selling phonographs and recording cylinders, he didn't imagine that this technology would compete with stage shows. He imagined it would become an arcade amusement or a home appliance like the phonograph. In 1889 he unveiled the Kinetoscope, a wooden box with a peephole on top. Inside the box were an electric light and a loop of film that was conveyed around some pulleys by cranking it.

Thomas Edison's Kinetoscope

Kinetoscopes did prove popular in arcades for a time, and Edison did offer a home version that presaged home video. At the time, there was a greater push for projectors, that would allow for multiple viewers to watch a single film in a theater. Magic lantern shows, which used projectors with still images on stained glass, had been around since the 17th century, so there was some precedent for this.

The first patent for a motion picture camera was filed in England by Louis Le Prince in 1888. Many others would make refinements, including Edison Company's W. K. L. Dickson, who created the kinetograph. Dickson split the standard 70 mm Eastman filmstock in two and added perforations on each side, creating the standard 35 mm filmstock. The perforations were made to accommodate the sprockets used in the kinetograph and kinetoscope.

After a falling out, Dickson and some of his coworkers left the Edison Company to form the competing American Mutoscope & Biograph Company. Edison unsuccessfully sued them for stealing the perforation and sprocket system. Unfortunately for Edison, he had failed to patent the system in Europe, and it became widely used by competitors there. By the time the lawsuit against Dickson's company got to court, the idea was considered standard technology. This was ultimately a very good thing because the standard mechanism allows films to be projected anywhere in the world.

Edison was also responsible for other major innovations that made film possible. Some of the earliest cameras and projectors were hand-cranked or ran on Edison batteries, but they were very inefficient. Edison's biggest contributions to the film industry may have been his work on electrical production and distribution. To be fair, people like George Westinghouse and Nikola Tesla contributed more in this area, but nonetheless, the film industry could not exist without the ability to run lights, projectors, cameras, and other relevant equipment on electricity.

While early kinetoscopes and similar devices relied on Edison's incandescent lamps, cameras could not. Filmstock was insensitive at the time and required film locations to be very brightly lit. Still photographers relied on a black powder flash, but that wouldn't work for movies because it wasn't continuous. In the early days of film, only the sun would provide enough light. For this reason, the pioneers of the industry would either film outside or build motion picture studios with skylights that could rotate to follow the sun.

Of course, neither sunlight nor weak incandescent bulbs were sufficient for projectors. From the turn of the century until 1970, carbon arc lights were used for cinema projectors because they were significantly brighter than any light bulb. Carbon arc lamps create light much like that of a stick welder. When two carbon electrodes get very close together, they create an electrical arc and a brilliant white light. The downside

Thomas Edison's rotating "Black Maria"
The first movie studio.

is that the carbon rods are consumed in the process and must be continually fed together to keep burning. The rods typically last a little more than an hour. During the golden age of film, that was plenty of time for a single reel of film. Two projectors would be used for a feature-length film, so while one reel was playing, the rods could be replaced on the other projector. In the 1970s, when reels were spliced together, and cinemas began using a single projector, the carbon arc lamps didn't last long enough. They were then replaced by the longer-lasting, but less energy efficient xenon arc lamps. Most of today's digital projectors continue to use xenon lamps, but the latest projectors now use lasers.

Manufacturing innovations were another necessity for the film industry. Eli Whitney's concept of "interchangeable parts" led to new manufacturing ideas in the late nineteenth and early twentieth centuries. Jigs to guide the machine tools, fixtures to hold workpieces in place, and blocks and gauges to check the accuracy of the finished parts allowed for the standardized mass production of film, cameras, projectors and other equipment and replacement parts.

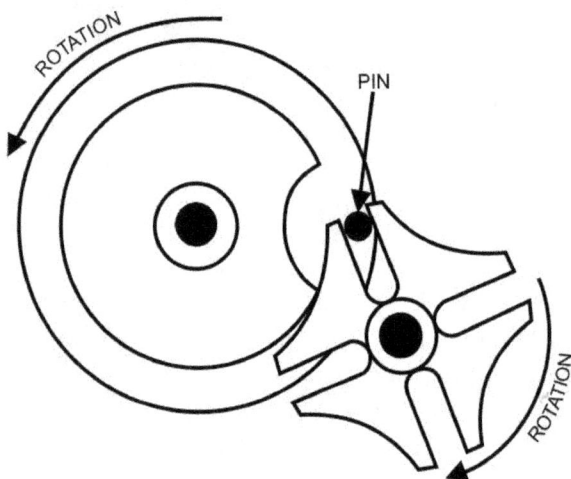

GENEVA GEAR
With each orbit of the pin, the Geneva gear makes a 1/4 turn.

One of the most significant innovations in camera and projector parts was the implementation of the "Geneva gear." Originally known as the "Geneva stop," this gear was first used by watchmakers to ensure that watches couldn't be over-wound. The gear moves forward in increments allowing a frame of film to stop in front of the lens for a split second before the next frame is advanced. This gives movies their flickering sound and look. If each frame didn't momentarily stop before the lens, the picture would be a complete blur. Initially a fan or "beater mechanism" was placed before the lens to simulate the momentary stop, but it wasn't very effective. In 1896, German inventor and movie mogul, Oskar Messter, modified the Geneva stop for use in projectors and it was widely adopted by the industry.

Once the basic concepts of film, cameras, and projectors were established, thousands of refinements would follow. The most sought-after innovation for film was sound. It was the greatest obstacle to film's being able to compete with live entertainment. There were many impediments to bringing sound to the motion picture, including: syncing the sound to the picture; amplification, so that it could be heard in an auditorium; deterioration of the recordings; fidelity to the original sound; extraneous noise in both recording and playback; and adjusting the sound quality for different theaters.

Silent films were often accompanied by local pianists or organists in theaters, but Thomas Edison believed he could replace those musicians with phonograph recordings. At first, he believed one could merely play a phonograph in coordination with a film to achieve the effect. Unfortunately, the phonographs quickly got out of sync with the film. Further, the phonographs had little or no amplification.

The first major breakthrough came in 1906 with Lee De Forest's invention of the amplifying audion vacuum tube. Originally intended for use with the telephone system, this device was used for public address systems and allowed sound to be heard in an auditorium at a reasonable volume. The race was then on to find the best recording and playback systems. There were many experiments in the 1910s, but practical solutions did not come until the 1920s.

Efforts were still being made to sync the sound on gramophone disks to film, but others wanted to put the sound directly on the film itself. This was accomplished by creating a light that would grow brighter and dimmer in relation to sound waves picked up by a microphone. The light, being fixed at the edge of the film frame, would expose the film to a greater or lesser extent as it ran through the camera. The process was reversed as the film ran through the projector. A light shining through the film onto a photosensor would be used to create sound when run through an amplifier. Throughout the twenties, this process was used for exhibitions and short films, but the quality of the sound was poor.

If the sound-on-film method was being used, it would be impossible to know if the sound quality was acceptable until after the film was developed, and in the case of sound-on-disk, the recording could not be played back without destroying the delicate wax master recording. So, a second wax recording was made at the same time to provide immediate confirmation that the recording went well.

Warner Brothers released the first sound feature film, *Don Juan* (1926). They used their "Vitaphone," synchronized sound-on-disk system, to achieve this, but the sound was simply an orchestration, contained no dialogue, and it was not tightly synchronized to the action onscreen. Then Warner Brothers released *The Jazz Singer* (1927), the first talking/singing feature film with synchronized sound, but even then, only a few parts of the film included talking and singing. It had a musical score, but mostly it had title cards like a silent film. Finally, the following year, Warner Brothers released the first "all talking" film, *Lights of New York* (1928).

The key to solving the synchronicity problem was to run the camera and recorders with the same motor. The motor and the recorders were in a room some distance from the set. When filming was to begin, someone on the stage would give the signal via intercom to start the motor. When the motor was started and up to speed, the person in the recording room would respond via intercom, "Speed." Then the director would call for the lights to be turned on, and the camera to begin rolling. Next, the assistant would "slate" the shot by announcing the scene and "take" number and snapping the clapperboard in front of the camera. The slap of the clapperboard would create a precise sound spike that could be aligned with the visual for better synchronization. Finally, the director would call for the action to begin. Motor, speed, lights, camera, slate, and action!

Filming from inside a soundproof booth.

Another major technical challenge was extraneous noise. In the early days of the silent era, a number of films could be shot simultaneously, side by side, in the same building to keep everything centrally located. With the implementation of sound, this was no longer possible. This is why the industry now refers to the buildings where films are shot as "soundstages." This is also why the noisy motors to run the camera and recording devices were in a separate building. On set, the cameras had to be housed in booths that limited their movement but controlled for noise. Location shooting beyond the backlot was virtually unheard of in the early days of sound because the equipment was bulky and there was no way to compensate for extraneous noise.

642 Cardiline Shotgun Microphone

The engineering of microphones began with the telephone industry and was later adapted for public address and radio. Still, those microphones did not have the fidelity, and directionality required for the movies. Engineers continued to make many new improvements to microphones for the film industry, and in 1963, Electro-Voice won an academy award for the "642 Cardiline shotgun microphone" which could virtually eliminate any sound that was not directly in front of it. New microphone

180

development continues to this day, with special emphasis on wireless microphones.

On the exhibition end of the sound film process, cinemas had to invest in soundproofing, as well as sound system equipment to play the films. These systems could be very expensive, but sound film was so popular that the theaters were quick to make the change. It was fortuitous that they did so early on because, after the stock market crash in October of 1929, funds dried up for that sort of investment. It was also fortunate that the studios and cinemas agreed to support both the sound-on-film, and sound-on-disk format to prevent cutthroat competition.

By the mid-thirties, the sound-on-disk method was abandoned, and sound-on-film had improved to the point that it became the preferred method. After the second world war, the studios began using magnetic tape for recording, which would ultimately be edited, synced, and turned into sound-on-film for the final product. In the 1950s, they tried placing a magnetic recording strip on the final celluloid film. This allowed for multiple sound channels that worked well with the widescreen cinema of the day, but it was expensive and deteriorated quickly after multiple showings.

As location filming became more popular, the Nagra recorder became the industry standard. Nagra is a brand of rugged, battery-operated, reel-to-reel recorders made with the precision of a Swiss watch. Keeping a consistent speed, while not stretching the magnetic tape was critical for professional synchronous recording. That, combined with its superior sound quality and light weight, made it the de facto recorder for the industry from the 1960s up through the 1990s, when digital recording became possible.

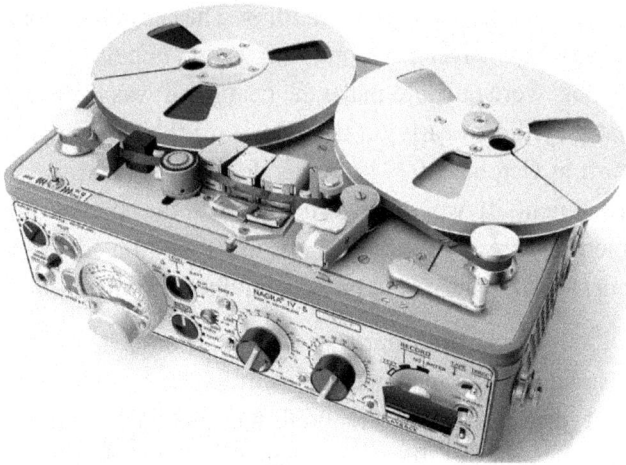

Nagra IV-S Recorder

Consistent sound quality from theater to theater remained a problem for the rest of the century. Dolby compression was created to reduce the hiss that was so prevalent in older films and to allow for a greater range of sound frequencies. The Dolby stereo sound system introduced in 1976 allowed four sound channels to be optically printed on film.

Then, in 1983 the THX sound standards were introduced. THX is a certification for recording and playback that assures constant quality for all participating films and theaters.

The first digital sound film, *Batman Returns* (1992), used Dolby Digital and *Jurassic Park* (1993) was the first film to use the DTS Inc., Digital Theater System. This was a throwback to the sound-on-disk system. Three compact discs accompanied the film and were synchronized via a time code optically printed on the film. Sony also created a digital surround system, at that time called SDDS, Sony Dynamic Digital Sound, which is a 7.1 surround sound system.

In the new millennium, films typically sported four different soundtracks so they could work for any theater's sound system. The left and right edges of the film print have the SDDS code, the Dolby code is printed between the sprockets on one side, the analog optical tracks are located next to that, and the DTS time code runs right next to the picture.

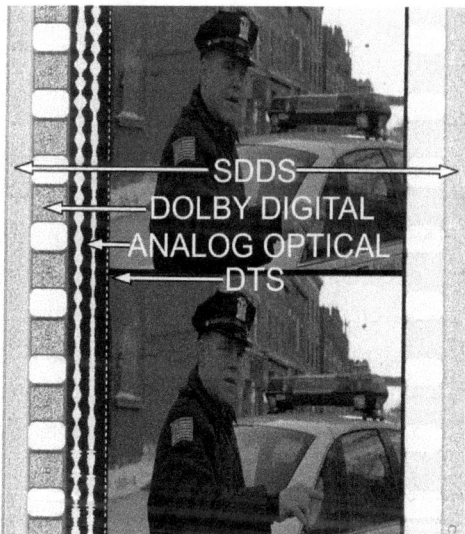

The Film Fan Handbook Volume 2

By 2015, the term "film" was largely an artifact, as nearly all motion pictures and cinemas are digital. Most motion pictures are delivered via computer hard disk or satellite, and the sound is included as a synchronized file.

Lenses, which have been around for more than 2,500 years, saw vast improvements as the fields of film and photography came of age in the twentieth century. Manufacturing precision, coatings, filters, mechanics, motors, electronics, and much more have been a part of lens innovation over the years.

The ability to "zoom" with a lens was one of the most important film innovations. While the concept had been used in telescopes for a hundred years, the zoom lens wouldn't see much use in the film industry until the 1940s. Unlike still photography that might employ a telephoto lens for a single picture, the "parfocal zoom" allows an image to stay in focus even while being magnified over the duration of a shot.

In 1952, Hollywood was looking to make widescreen color spectacles to battle the increased competition from small-screen black and white television. Released by the Cinerama Production Corporation, the aptly-titled documentary, *This is Cinerama* (1952) was the first such film. The Cinerama process involved three side by side synchronous cameras on the set and three synchronous side by side projectors in the cinema as well as an enormous curved screen and 7-channel surround sound.

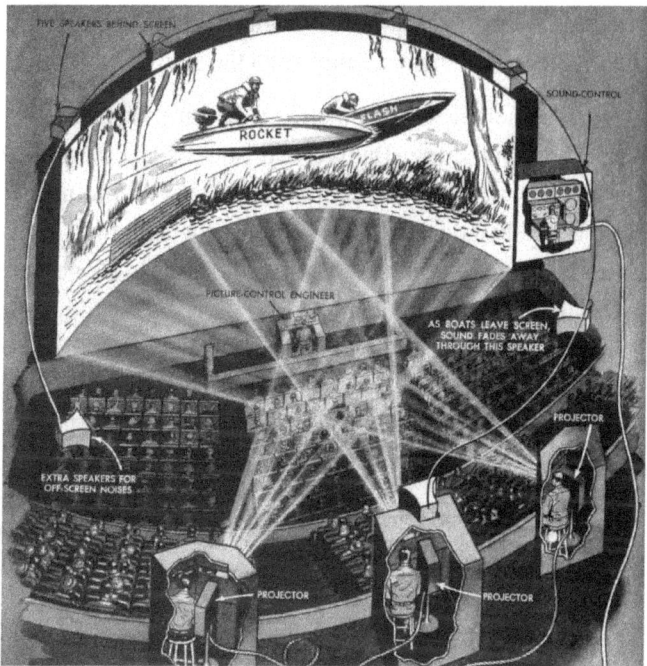

Cinerama

The following year, the first CinemaScope film, *The Robe* (1953), was distributed by Twentieth Century Fox. CinemaScope used anamorphic lenses for both the camera and projector. The camera lens would squeeze a wide-angle picture on to the standard 35mm film, and then the projector lens would reverse that process at the theater. The result was good but not perfect. Because the concept was to put more picture onto a standard piece of film, the resolution wasn't great and it was very grainy when projected, but in time, better filmstock corrected for this. Close-up shots in CinemaScope also produced a

185

"mumps" effect; as the camera came in close to a subject, the image would distort, bulging to the sides.

Nonetheless, CinemaScope became very popular, but lens manufacturer Bausch and Lomb had a hard time keeping up with the production of lenses. Soon, a new company, Panavision, stepped in to fill the need. Panavision grew (in part by acquisition) to be the preeminent supplier of cameras and lenses in the industry. Panavision works on a rental basis, which allows them to constantly improve and maintain the quality of their equipment – something that would be a liability for the studios if they owned the equipment outright.

VistaVision is another widescreen process that was used primarily by Paramount Pictures beginning in 1954. VistaVision cameras and projectors ran 35 mm film "sideways." This allowed the frame to be twice as wide as a standard 35 mm print while maintaining the same aspect ratio. It did not have the same distortion or quality problems CinemaScope had, but it had other problems. Because the frame was doubled, the speed had to be doubled as well, and it required twice as much filmstock, making it very expensive. Most often the prints were downsized for standard 35 mm projectors. The quality was superior, though, and it was sometimes used for high-quality special effects shots into the 21st century.

There's another way to produce a bigger movie; use bigger film. The Todd-AO process used a 65 mm negative filmstock, and 70 mm filmstock for the final product to accommodate a magnetic soundtrack. Todd-

AO was a joint effort between Broadway producer Mike Todd and the American Optical Company of Buffalo, New York.

Beginning with *Oklahoma!* (1955), Todd-AO used the higher frame rate of 30 frames per second versus the traditional 24 per second. This proved to be a problem. Most theaters didn't accommodate widescreen formats, and the films had to be scaled down to a standard 35 mm, 24 fps, format for wide distribution. How do you turn a 30 fps film into a 24 fps film? You don't – at least not with 1950s technology. Oklahoma! was shot twice. The performers did the scene once for the Todd-AO camera, and then after the camera was switched out for a CinemaScope camera, they would do the scene again. In the end, there were two completely different versions of the film with different editing and soundtracks. The Todd-AO version runs eight minutes longer than the CinemaScope version. The Todd-AO version is considered superior because the performances are fresh. After waiting around for the camera switch, the performers grew weary. Unfortunately, most people saw the CinemaScope version because the 24 fps rate was standard. Only recently has the Todd-AO version been available on Blu-ray disc.

Todd-AO went on to make twenty-one more films in 65/70 mm format, but they were done at 24 fps. By the 1970s, Todd-AO switched to a less expensive anamorphic 35 mm format like CinemaScope. In the late 1980s, Todd-AO could no longer compete with

Panavision and evolved into a sound post-production company.

There were other attempts at widescreen cinema. They went by names like, "Megascope," "Vistascope," "Naturama," "Cinemagic," "Lunarscope," "Terrorscope," "Metroscope," "Widevision," "Superama," "VastVision," and "Cinepanscope." Obviously, some were trying to exploit confusion with other trade names, and some were just silly. Some did use anamorphic lenses like CinemaScope, which proved to be the most cost-effective way to create a widescreen movie because it could be made with standard film, using a single standard camera, and be exhibited with a standard projector. Only the lenses needed to be changed. Others were films shot in the traditional 35mm format and simply blown up for a large screen, meaning that the resolution was terrible.

Hercules Against the Moon Men (1964)
in "Cosmic Color and Lunarscope"

Chapter Eleven - Technology

For the most part, a larger screen is a gimmick. The optimum viewing angle for a film is when there are 36 degrees to the edges of the screen. So, to view a larger screen properly you need to be further away from the screen, which makes the screen look smaller. Still, the large screen trend persists with Imax theaters, which turn 70mm film on its side to provide the greatest resolution of any common film format. On the other hand, large screen technology led to some other ideas, such as surround sound, better lens technology, and new aspect ratios that would be used in high definition video.

Color had been part of film from the earliest days. In the nineteenth century, films were very short and were hand colored frame by frame. Then, to speed up the process for more prints, Pathé invented a process where stencils could be cut for the films and then run through a machine that would dye each film print one color at a time. Both processes were time-consuming, expensive, and not practical for feature-length films.

By the 1920s, films were either tinted (the entire frame was dyed a color) or toned (only the dark silver parts of the print were dyed) to express the general mood of a scene. This proved to be far more trouble and expense than was necessary, and it was incompatible with the sound-on-film technology.

The perception of color works by stimulating the "cone" cells in the back of the eye. There are three types of cone cells, ones that are stimulated by short wavelengths (violet/blue), ones that are stimulated by medium wavelengths (green), and ones that are stimulated by long wavelengths (red). Pigment uses a subtractive color model, meaning that by combining cyan, yellow, and magenta pigment, any color can be obtained. Mixing even amounts of all three colors produces black pigment. Light uses an additive color model, meaning that by combining red, blue, and green light, any color can be obtained. Mixing even amounts of all three colors produces white light.

The first attempts at practical color film were using an additive method. The Kinemacolor method was used from 1908-1914. Red and green filters (which are technically yellow-magenta and yellow-cyan respectively) were alternately placed in front of the lens via the use of a color wheel. When filming, the result was a black and white film in which every other frame was filtered for red or green. When shown through a projector that also had a red/green color wheel, a color image was presented. There were three problems with this system. First, the film had to run at twice the normal speed to prevent the color from flickering, secondly, it didn't work well with fast-moving action for the same reason, and third, there was no blue color. If blue were added to the color wheel, the film would have to run at three times the normal speed, which was not practical at the time.

In 1911, William Freese-Greene developed the Biocolour process, which was very much like the Kinemacolor process, but instead of using a color wheel in the projector, every other frame was dyed either red or green. This allowed the film to be presented with the use of a standard projector. Unfortunately, the process still had the same inherent problems that Kinemacolor had.

Technicolor began in 1916 with the same sort of additive color process (later known as Process 1 Technicolor) but abandoned it in 1922 in favor of a subtractive process (Process 2 Technicolor). Rather than using a color wheel, Technicolor used a beam splitter that would allow the same image to be exposed on two strips of negative film. One image passed through a red filter and the other a green filter. The red filtered negative was then toned cyan and the green filtered negative was toned magenta. When the two negatives were glued together, they could be run through the standard projector. This process eliminated the color flickering and the need to run the film at double speed. There was still no blue.

In 1928, a new Technicolor process was used (Process 3 Technicolor). The process was similar to the old one, but now used a method called "imbibing." This would essentially use the two negatives to imprint dye on a third blank filmstrip. This produced a much richer image that could still be run through a regular projector, but once again there was no blue.

Color was a very expensive process, so by the time the Great Depression came in the 1930s, the studios were more interested in exploiting sound than color. The quality of black-and-white filmstock had improved to the point that audiences didn't demand color film.

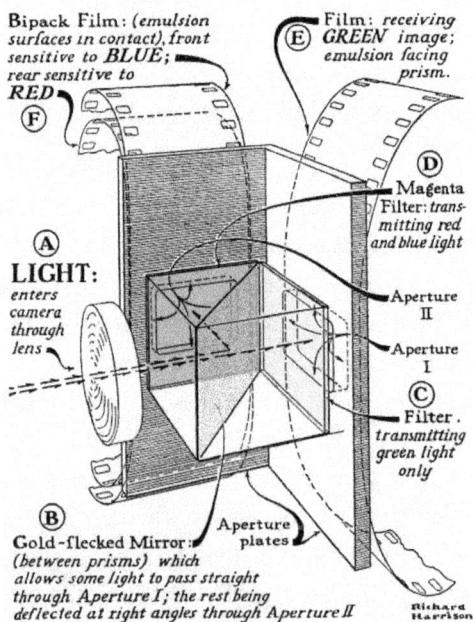

Process 4 Technicolor

Nonetheless, Technicolor developed yet another process in 1932 (Process 4 Technicolor). This new process was like the old one, but at last, it added blue to the pallet. After the light passed through the beam splitter one-third of the light went through the green filter as before, but the other two-thirds went through a magenta filter, which absorbed green light and allowed the red and blue thirds of the spectrum to pass. There were two strips of film behind this filter. The front one was only sensitive to short wavelengths of light and thus captured the blue spectrum. The long wavelengths passed through to the second film strip that was only sensitive to the red spectrum. The three strips would then be used in the imbibing process to dye the final film.

Disney was the earliest adopter of this process. They began using it for their cartoon shorts in 1932. The first feature film to use this process was RKO Radio Picture's *Becky Sharp* (1935). The following two years had six Technicolor features each. Then in 1938, there were thirteen Technicolor films including *The Adventures of Robin Hood* (1938), with its brilliant, award-winning color. Sound was standard by that point, and Hollywood was once again excited to embrace color.

Technicolor was a very expensive and complicated process. Because their reputation was on the line, the Technicolor company insisted on controlling every aspect of the process. Not only did Technicolor require the use of special cameras and trained camera operators, but it also required special Technicolor makeup

193

applied by a Technicolor makeup artist. A Technicolor supervisor had to be employed to make certain that costumes and sets would look good on screen. The process also required expensive lighting that was exceedingly bright, triple the length of negative film, and an expensive dye transfer process. Technicolor was clearly only practical for big-budget films.

As far back as the 1930s, Agfa (a German company), Fuji (a Japanese company), and Eastman Kodak (an American company), had all been working on a three-emulsion layer film that would capture color on a single negative. In fact, they had developed color film that worked well for still photos, slides, and home movies, but it was far too grainy for the motion picture industry. Technicolor did occasionally use a "monopack," three-emulsion layer film for travelogues and location shooting for films like *Lassie Come Home* (1943), because the cameras were lighter and more portable, but the quality (particularly the contrast) wasn't great.

The first quality monopack 35 mm color motion picture negative film was Kodak's Eastmancolor, which was introduced in 1950. While the quality was not as good as the three-strip Technicolor method, it was certainly sufficient, and less expensive. Eastmancolor could be used in a standard camera and required no advisors, special makeup, camera operators, or anything else. In fact, even Technicolor began using Eastmancolor filmstock in 1955. There was one giant problem with Eastmancolor that hadn't been anticipated: the color fades over time. The cyan and yellow layers were particularly vulnerable, turning many old films a magenta color.

With Eastmancolor filmstock, the studio could process the film for themselves. However, if they didn't adhere to strict Eastman standards, it couldn't be called Eastmancolor. Adjusting the time of exposure to achieve the desired consistent look, a process referred to as "color timing" or "color grading," could be very challenging. So,

195

the studios gave the processing their own brand name, such as Metrocolor (MGM), Warnercolor, Deluxe (Twentieth Century Fox), Columbiacolor, Pathécolor, etc. Technicolor was still using its dye transfer process until 1974. It produced great results, but it was too expensive and slow.

Many small budget films were still shot in black and white through the early 1960s. It had become the custom by that point and was even a hallmark of some genres, like direct cinema. However, by 1967, most movies were shot in color. It is hardly a coincidence that sales for color televisions surpassed the sales of black and white televisions that year, and that more than half of the television programming was in color.

While computers had been used in filmmaking as far back as the early 1970s, the film industry in the 1990s (like nearly every other industry) saw a remarkable shift in technology. Not only were computers used for computer-generated imagery, but for cameras and camera movement, editing, sound recording, project management, finance, supply chain, human resources, communication, recording and projection, etcetera. Indeed, while the term "motion picture" remains applicable today, the term "film" belongs to a bygone era.

KEY POINTS:

- Film is the only art form that requires the use of technology to both create it and experience it.
- Early on, the industry was more concerned with owning technology rights than film content.
- Film began not as a single invention but as a confluence of developments.
- Film traces its roots to persistence-of-vision toys and innovations in photography.
- The first photographic motion picture happened when Eadweard Muybridge set up a series of still cameras to capture the movement of a horse and then projected those images using a zoopraxiscope.
- George Eastman patented the first practical perforated film rolls.
- In 1889, Thomas Edison invented the Kinetoscope, a wooden box with an electric light, a loop of film, and a peephole on top.
- Kinetoscopes were popular in arcade amusements, but unlike magic lantern shows, they were not able to project a film for a large audience.
- In 1888, Louis Le Prince patented the first motion picture camera.

- W. K. L. Dickson split the standard 70 mm Eastman film stock in two and added perforations on each side, creating the standard 35 mm film stock.
- Film would not be possible without the electrical power system created by Thomas Edison, George Westinghouse and Nikola Tesla.
- Early filmstock was insensitive and thus only the sun was bright enough to light a scene.
- From the turn of the century until 1970, carbon arc lights were used for cinema projectors.
- The carbon arc lights were replaced with less energy efficient xenon arc lamps and later lasers.
- Manufacturing innovations, including the mass production of standardized parts, were another necessity for the film industry.
- Oskar Messter's modified "Geneva gear" allows film to stop in front of the lens for a split second to prevent blurring.
- The most sought-after innovation for film was sound.
- Edison believed pianists or organists in theaters could be replaced with phonographs, but they quickly got out of synch and did not have amplification.

- In 1906, Lee De Forest's invented the audion vacuum tube which permitted amplified theater sound.
- The audion was also used to create and play sound waves printed on the film.
- It was impossible to know if the sound-on-film method was working until the film was developed, and a sound-on-disk recording could not be played back without destroying the delicate wax master.
- "Vitaphone," a synchronized sound-on-disk system, was used for accompaniment for the first sound feature film, *Don Juan* (1926) and the first talking/singing feature film, *The Jazz Singer* (1927).
- The key to solving the synchronicity problem was to run the camera and recorders with the same motor.
- Sound films had to be shot on soundstages to keep out extraneous noise.
- The 642 Cardiline shotgun microphone became the standard in film because it could virtually eliminate any sound that was not directly in front of it.
- Today, miniature wireless microphones are sometimes used to supplement the shotgun microphone.

- In the 1920s, cinemas had to make a significant investment to install sound systems, but it proved to be a good investment.
- After World War II, studios began using magnetic tape to record sound, and they even tried placing a magnetic recording strip on the final celluloid film, but it was expensive and deteriorated quickly.
- By the 1960s, Nagra, a brand of rugged, battery-operated, reel-to-reel recorders that keep a consistent speed without stretching the magnetic tape, became the de facto recorder for the industry.
- Dolby compression was created to reduce the hiss and the Dolby stereo sound system allowed four sound channels to be optically printed on film.
- In 1983, THX a certification that assures constant quality for recording and playback was introduced.
- Dolby Digital, first used for *Batman Returns* (1992), was the first digital sound system.
- The Digital Theater System, created by DTS Inc., uses three compact discs for sound that are synchronized with the movie via time codes optically printed on the film.

- Sony created a 7.1 digital surround sound system called Sony Dynamic Digital Sound or SDDS.
- Eventually, filmstock would incorporate four different soundtracks: SDDS, Dolby, the analog optical tracks, and the DTS time code.
- Since 2015, nearly all motion pictures are digital, and the sound is delivered as a synchronous digital file.
- Lenses have been improving for more than 2,500 years.
- The "parfocal zoom" allows an image to stay in focus even while being magnified over the duration of a shot.
- In the 1950s, Hollywood made widescreen color spectacles to compete with small-screen black and white television.
- The first widescreen movie was *This is Cinerama* (1952).
- Cinerama used three cameras, three projectors, a curved screen, and 7-channel surround sound.
- CinemaScope used anamorphic lenses that would squeeze a wide-angle picture onto standard filmstock and then expand the picture again when projected.

- While there was distortion with early anamorphic lenses they got better over time.
- As demand grew, Panavision was successful at renting cameras and lenses.
- VistaVision cameras and projectors ran 35 mm film "sideways," to have a wider frame, but the film had to run twice as fast.
- The Todd-AO widescreen process used a 65 mm negative film stock, and 70 mm stock for the final product to accommodate a magnetic soundtrack.
- Other attempts at widescreen cinema were trying to exploit confusion with trade names, and often the quality was poor.
- The size of the screen is unimportant provided it is proportional to the distance the viewer sits from the screen.
- The earliest attempts at color film used stencils, dye, and spinning color wheels.
- Process 1 Technicolor was an additive color process that used a color wheel and dye.
- Process 2 Technicolor was subtractive and used a beam splitter and two strips of film for red and green colors.

- Process 3 Technicolor was similar to Process 2 but used a two-strip imbibing process to dye a third blank strip of film.
- Process 4 Technicolor was similar to Process 3, but had three colors red, green, and blue.
- To make sure the color was perfect, the Technicolor company insisted that a supervisor be hired to oversee every aspect of the filmmaking process.
- In 1950, Kodak introduced Eastmancolor, the first quality monopack, three-emulsion layer film.
- "Color timing" or "color grading," is the challenging process of adjusting exposure time to achieve a consistent look.
- Each studio gave their timing process a unique brand name such as Metrocolor (MGM), Warnercolor, Deluxe (Twentieth Century Fox), Columbiacolor, Pathécolor, etc.
- Many small budget films were shot in black and white through the early 1960s.
- By 1967, when color became standard for television, most movies were shot in color too.
- By the 1990s computers were used for nearly every aspect of filmmaking.
- The term "film" is an artifact.

CHAPTER TWELVE

EFFECTS

Life imitates art, and art imitates life, but art isn't real; it's strictly imitation. Film, as an art, is completely phony. It's all an illusion. Audience members sitting in a cinema have their senses stimulated by the light and sound of things that aren't really there. Indeed, most of what is seen within each of the 150,000 frames of a feature film is fake in some way too. The walls are flimsy, the rain comes from sprinklers, the elegant costumes are haphazardly stitched together, and the jewels are made of plastic. Effects are the filmmaker's "tricks of the trade." They are the magical part of "movie magic."

It takes many effects that create the overall illusion of film, and they fit into three main categories: special effects, visual effects, and sound effects, but even those categories can be subdivided into various types of effects. This can be quite confusing. As technology changes, the names for these effects change too, and sometimes the names will be appropriated for new effects. For example, what was once referred to as "visual effects" is now usually called "optical effects," and the term "visual effects" now means something completely different. What was once called "engineering effects," "mechanical effects," or "gags" are often now called "practical effects," but the term "practical effects" doesn't mean what it did originally either.

The first special effect in film history is thought to be Alfred Clark's *The Execution of Mary, Queen of Scots* (1895). This thirteen-second film shows an executioner raise his axe to behead the monarch. For the effect, the film is edited and the actress playing Mary is replaced by a mannequin. The mannequin is then decapitated, and the executioner triumphantly holds the severed head aloft. The illusion is quite nice considering the technology of the time.

The Execution of Mary, Queen of Scots (1895)

The effects in early films were dubbed "special effects" only in retrospect. The first use of the term "special effect" was in 1939 when the Academy of

Motion Picture Arts and Sciences awarded an Oscar for "special effects in photography and sound." Remarkably, while the spectacular Oscar-winning films *Gone with the Wind* (1939) and *The Wizard of OZ* (1939) came out that year, the award went to E. H. Hansen (sound), and Fred Sersen (photographic) for the film, *The Rains Came* (1939).

The Rains Came (1939)

Today the term "special effects" refers to either "optical effects" or "practical effects." Both of these are effects that happen during principal filming. The above example, *The Execution of Mary, Queen of Scots* contains both a practical and an optical effect. The edit to replace the actress's body with the dummy is an optical effect.

The dummy itself (with a detachable head) is a practical effect.

Practical effects are any physical or mechanical illusion done in front of the camera during filming. "Practical" in this case connotes functionality, not pragmatism. For example, there is a long barroom brawl in *Shane* (1953), where tables and chairs are broken, and bottles are smashed over people's heads. Those elements function; they were intentionally constructed to break easily, so in film jargon, they would be referred to as "practicals." They are distinguished from the other bottles and tables that are merely there for set dressing.

Shane (1953)

Atmospherics would also be considered practical effects. Lightning, rain, fog, and snow are frequently seen in film, but they can be difficult to control. Filmmakers certainly can't rely on Mother Nature to provide the rightatmosphere. For example, snow scene could only be shot in the winter, on a day that not only has snow but has the right kind of snow in the right place for the purposes of the film.

Even simple rain effects can be a challenge to create believably. Sprinkler heads must be lofted 30 feet into the air so that droplets have time to fall straight, and they need to be very large drops if they are to be perceived on film. A lightning effect is often accomplished by throwing aluminum dust into a propane flame. Snow has been created using ice, corn flakes, plastic, foam, and even chicken feathers, but the biggest challenge has always been to find something that will melt slowly in close-up shots under hot lights. Wind can be a challenge if sound is to be captured, because not only do large fans make noise, but the blowing wind itself will be picked up on microphones. Fans also tend to blow debris into the camera at inopportune moments.

Fog can be created with dry ice (frozen carbon dioxide) or "fog juice" (water and glycerin), but those methods are not reliable. Titanium tetrachloride, which is used by skywriters as well as the military for smokescreens, is used more often because it's quite thick, stays close to the ground, and doesn't dissipate quickly. Used with restraint, this can also create a nearly imperceptible haze that will diffuse light and give a scene a softer, sentimental feel. This is sometimes called the "Spielberg effect" because director Stephen Spielberg uses it in many of his movies. In the film, *Lincoln* (2012), for example, the eponymous president stands alone and thoughtful while his office is oddly filled with a sentimental fog.

Lincoln (2012)

Of course, Hollywood loves explosions, stunts, gunfire, and blood, all of which are practical effects. Because these things are as dangerous as they are spectacular, they require the use of experts. Remarkably, while pyrotechnic manufacturers are licensed by the Bureau of Alcohol, Tobacco, Firearms and Explosives, pyrotechnicians themselves are only licensed (when required) by state and local authorities. Stuntmen, who are often in the middle of these dangerous situations, usually train at a school or have military, athletic, or circus experience, but they are not required to have any other qualifications. Sometimes they belong to organizations such as the Society of American Fight Directors, and typically they belong to the Screen Actors Guild.

The Great Train Robbery (1903)

Guns have been a part of motion pictures dating at least as far back as *The Great Train Robbery* (1903), when actor Justice T. Barnes, dressed as a cowboy, famously startled audiences by firing his gun directly at them. The handling of guns and creating believable gunfire can be very dangerous, and in large productions an armorer will be hired to oversee the use of weapons. Rubber "dummy" guns and other weapons are most commonly used in filmmaking, but so-called "function guns," which have moving parts (but don't actually fire) are used for close-ups. Sharpshooters firing live rounds were sometimes used in early moviemaking, and ricochet shots were accomplished with marbles, chalk, or dirt propelled by sling shot. Later, "blank" gunfire, paintball guns, and small pyrotechnic "squibs" were preferred, but today, much of this is computer generated.

It's a Wonderful Life (1946)

Where there are weapons, there's blood. It can seep, drip, squirt, spray, splatter or slowly flow into a puddle. In the golden age of Hollywood, when the production code was in force, characters rarely bled. In most noir films and old westerns, the gunshot victims simply grabbed their supposedly injured body part and crumpled over. Occasionally, incidental blood would be seen, such as when the character George Baily cuts his lip in *It's a Wonderful Life* (1946), but it was kept very subtle. When films were made in black and white, chocolate syrup was a very effective analog for blood. Chocolate syrup was even used for the famous shower slashing in *Psycho* (1960). However, while the production code was in force in the United States until 1968, there were no such constraints in Europe. Beginning with *The Curse of Frankenstein* (1957), Hammer Film Productions in England began turning out color horror movies that were quite graphic (for the time), and other producers soon followed suit. Of course, chocolate syrup wouldn't work for color film, so effects artists everywhere began concocting their own secret recipe. The most famous, a line of fake blood called "Kensington Gore," was concocted by British pharmacist, John Tynegate. "Kensington Gore" (named after a neighborhood in London) is now a generic term for all stage blood. It comes in many shades and consistencies (such as aged, venal, clotting, and arterial) to fill various needs. For example, sometimes it needs to be thin enough to flow through tubing, sometimes it needs to stay liquid under hot movie lights, sometimes it needs to be edible, and sometimes it needs to explode with the use of pyrotechnic squibs.

Naturally, where there's blood, there are wounds, and that's the responsibility of the makeup effects department. Makeup was important to film early on. During the silent era, orthochromatic film stock was used, and it didn't allow for subtle gradations of gray. Everything red looked black on film, and everything blue looked white. This is why actors in silent films seem to have pasty white faces and black lips. It's not the makeup, it's the film stock.

In 1914, Max Factor invented a new kind of makeup to compensate for this, and the discipline of movie makeup was born. Then actor Lon Chaney, "the man of a thousand faces," took movie makeup to a new level. Chaney became famous for inventing new makeup

Holbrook Blinn and Mary Pickford, *Rosita* (1923)
filmed with orthochromatic film stock.

techniques that would completely alter his appearance. In
fact, in *Outside the Law* (1920), Chaney played both the
heroic Chinese servant, Ah Wing, as well as the
murderous Black Mike Sylva who shoots Wing. Chaney
would eventually become famous for his eponymous
portrayals of *The Hunchback of Notre Dame* (1923), and
The Phantom of the Opera (1925), both of which
employed groundbreaking makeup effects. Then makeup
artist Jack Pierce made cultural history with his
transformation of Boris Karloff into the monster in
Frankenstein (1931). The creature's heavy brow and flat
head led to more creative uses of makeup, such as the
panoply of strange characters in *The Wizard of Oz* (1939).
Foam rubber and latex appliances became commonplace

in the 1950s' "creature features," and would remain so for the rest of the century. For *The Exorcist* (1973) makeup artist Dick Smith combined mechanical effects with makeup effects to create the horror of a young girl possessed by a demon. Soon makeup, practical effects, puppetry, and animatronics would be combined routinely.

Die Nibelungen: Siegfried (1924)

Puppetry is one of the oldest practical effects in film, and Georges Méliès once again gets credit for introducing it to the medium. In *The Witch* (1906), Méliès used giant frog, and owl puppets, as well as a couple of puppets that look like tadpoles and a fire-breathing dragon. Then German filmmaker Fritz Lang created a 60-foot-long fire-breathing dragon puppet for his film, *Die Nibelungen: Siegfried* (1924). Of course, the greatest innovator of movie puppetry was Jim Henson, who created the first feature-length film with a puppet (Muppet) universe, *The Muppet Movie* (1979).

Animatronics effectively replaces puppetry with robotics. The first true animatronics were the singing animatronic birds in Disneyland's "Enchanted Tiki Room" exhibit which opened in June of 1963. At that same time, Disney used another animatronic bird, a robin, in the filming of *Mary Poppins* (1964). From there, animatronics continually improved with technology. Director Stephen Spielberg would famously take animatronics underwater to create the shark in *Jaws* (1975), and then go on to use animatronics in *E.T. the Extraterrestrial* (1982) and *Jurassic Park* (1993). Animatronics can be operated by a puppeteer, a computer, or a combination of both. The main advantage of animatronics is that it can create an inhuman character that performers can interact with. The main disadvantage is that the mechanical nature of animatronics can make them clunky and unreliable. One of the most artistically remarkable uses of animatronics was the creature from *Alien* (1979), which was performed by an extremely tall, thin costumed actor wearing an animatronic head.

Optical effects, like practical effects, are created while filming. They can be thought of as optical illusions for film. As in the example of *The Execution of Mary, Queen of Scots* (1895), optical effects can be as simple as a film edit or be achieved "in camera" with things like special lenses, filters or double exposures.

For example, part of the frame can be masked off as the film runs through the camera, and then the film can be rewound, so the masked off area can be exposed, and the previously exposed area can be masked off. This can create myriad illusions such as the same actor appearing simultaneously in more than one place on the screen. Once again, Goerges Mélies made use of this effect as far back as the nineteenth century. In *The Four Troublesome Heads* (1898) he replicates his own head three times, to form a sort of singing quartet (even though it's a silent film).

The Four Troublesome Heads (1898)

Another optical effect is the "rear projection" or "process" shot. The concept for this type of shot seems straightforward; the action is simply filmed in front of a movie screen. This is most often seen in driving

Obvious rear projection shot in *Dr. No* (1962)

sequences where actors are filmed in a stationary car on a soundstage while the filmed background moves behind them. It sounds simple, but this sort of effect can be a challenge to produce. In fact, the technology did not exist for this type of shot until the 1930s, and even then, the effect is unconvincing in many films. To begin with, the projected scene needs to be shot well in advance of the principal filming, and the filmmakers need to anticipate what the scene will look like to keep the background images in scale with the actors who will be standing in front of it. Next, the effect requires a very large soundstage, so the projector has enough distance to create a large image on a large screen. The film stock used for the projected image must also be of sufficient quality, and it must be projected with a lamp bright enough that it won't be washed out by the lights illuminating the actors. If the actors are placed too close to the screen their shadows will fall on it. If the actors are far in front of the screen, they're easier to light, but then the screen must be even larger and brighter, and the camera lens needs to be able to focus on both the foreground and background. Finally, the projector and the camera must be in sync so that the camera does not capture the projection in the middle of changing a frame.

Forced perspective shots are another optical illusion that's been frequently used in films. Because the camera has only one "eye" it has no depth perception. Thus, with the proper lens, the camera can be fooled when objects near the camera are in the same focal plane as those that are far from the camera. The result is that something small can appear quite large, and something large can appear quite small relative to other elements in the scene. Imagine, for example, that a bug was to crawl across the lens of the camera. It would look gargantuan in comparison to an actor standing ten feet in front of the camera. An excellent example of this is *Darby O'Gill and the Little People* (1959). In that film, scenes are shared between full-sized characters and diminutive leprechauns. However, all the characters are played by actors of average stature. By having the actors playing the leprechauns 4 times farther away from the camera, they appear ¼ the size of the other actors on screen. The reverse was done for *Attack of the 50 Foot Woman* (1958) where the eponymous woman towered over the other actors.

Miniature effects use scale models to save time and money. They are particularly useful in creating scenes of massive devastation, such as the crumbling buildings in *Earthquake* (1974) or when the camera needs to fly through a setting. For example, models of spaceships were used extensively in *2001: A Space Odyssey* (1968) to replicate a journey through the universe.

Darby O'Gill and the Little People (1959)

The term "miniature" can be a little misleading. Some models can be quite large to accommodate cameras and equipment. It is also necessary because the texture and physics of materials don't scale well. For example, you can't just use a smaller piece of wood for a door, because the grain would be the wrong scale. Other elements such as water or fire are physically impossible to scale down because a lower quantity of water or a smaller flame will behave differently in relation to other scaled-down aspects of the scene. The speed of the motion must be scaled down as well. Miniatures are usually shot in high speed, which makes everything appear in slow motion in the final effect. When film runs faster through a camera, it creates more frames for the scene. Then, when it is run through a projector at regular speed, the extra frames make the scene longer, creating a slow-motion effect. This alters the viewer's sense of physics. For example, a miniature rock tumbling down a miniature hill will seem to move unusually quickly at regular speed, but when done in slow motion, it will seem natural.

Miniatures can be combined with live action through something called the Schüfftan process. A mirror is placed at a 45° angle in front of the camera and a model placed to the side of the camera is reflected in it. When a portion of the reflective coating on the mirror is scratched away turning it into clear glass, the live action beyond it can be seen as if looking through a window. The net effect in the camera viewfinder is live action taking place in a model.

A similar process, called a glass shot, is achieved by simply filming through a sheet of glass that has been partially painted with a background image. This is usually done for large vista shots. For example, in *The Adventures of Robin Hood* (1938) there is a wide shot of Robin and his Merry Men approaching a castle. The top half of the screen, depicting the castle, is painted on glass, but the actors in the foreground can be seen traveling down the road at the bottom of the screen. The challenge in creating this sort of shot is blending the color and lighting so that the painting and live action match.

The Adventures of Robin Hood (1938)

Both the Schüfftan process and the glass shot are old-school examples of "matte shots," whose basic principle is to composite two or more images onto a single frame of film. This concept was improved upon in the 1930s using visual effects.

Visual effects are created after the principle shooting has been completed. The principle tool for this is the optical printer. An optical printer is essentially a copying machine for film. It has a projector at one end of the machine and a camera on the other with a screen in between. The camera simply films the image projected on the screen and makes a copy. This is how prints of a film used to be made for distribution, but it's a useful tool for creating effects too. For example, a painted piece of glass can be inserted to create the same effect as a glass shot, or several masked shots can be composited to create a single image. Likewise, a filter can be placed in front of the camera to change the hue, saturation, or luminance of a film.

An Optical Printer

"Day for night" shooting can be accomplished this way. Filming night scenes can be a challenge because, without light, the film will just look black. The solution for this is to film the night scene in full light, and then underexpose the film and use a filter to alter the color in the optical printer. A suitable result is difficult to achieve, but it's become such a standard technique that audiences generally accept the convention.

Through a very complicated process, a "traveling matte" can be created. This is where the matte moves or changes in each frame of the film instead of being a single stationary painted picture. Typically, an actor or an object will be filmed in front of a blue or green screen, and then using filters, the green or blue areas will be left unexposed on the final film and the reverse will be done for the background image. When the foreground object is combined with the background, the effect is complete. *Star Wars: Episode IV - A New Hope* (1977), won an Oscar for Best Visual Effects for its extensive use of models and traveling mattes.

There is a myriad of tricks and techniques that have been created using the optical printer including animation, but variations on the matte shot comprise the principle technique. By using mattes to mask parts of the screen, and printing and reprinting, nearly anything is possible.

Animation is another sort of optical effect. Using the same matte process animated elements can be added to live action films. Think of the sparks that fly from the ruby slippers in *The Wizard of Oz* (1939) or the menacing birds in Alfred Hitchcock's *The Birds* (1963). These effects are achieved by simply placing a series of drawings inked on clear cellulose acetate (cels) into an optical printer. The drawings are then photographed one at a time, and once they are captured on film and run through a projector in sequence, they create the illusion of animated movement. This is the same principle used for "classic" or "fully produced" animation, like *Snow White and the Seven Dwarfs* (1937).

Rotoscoping is a similar type of animation, but in this case, an animator draws the cels over top of live-action footage. This captures natural movements and proportions that are inherent to live action, but it has the visual appearance of animation. One of the most spectacular examples of this is *Loving Vincent* (2017). In this case, a cast of more than 30 actors performed for the camera to tell a story about Vincent Van Gogh. Then 125 fine art painters were hired to paint over that action frame by frame in the style of Van Gogh and combine it with background paintings based on Van Gogh's work. The result is an interesting mix of action that seems quite realistic even while it is represented in Van Gogh's imaginative style.

On the left, actress Eleanor Tomlinson, in the center, Van Gogh's painting of Adeline Ravoux, and on the right, the rotoscoped version of Eleanor Tomlinson as Adeline Ravoux in *Loving Vincent* (2017).[9]

Another technique is stop-motion animation. It involves shooting a film one frame at a time while moving objects (often clay models) slightly between each frame. The first stop-motion film, *The Humpty Dumpty Circus* (1897) was created using articulated toys. (Unfortunately, that film has been lost.) Stop motion would ultimately be perfected and combined with live-action. The most notable stop-motion animators were Willis O'Brien, who created *King Kong* (1933), George Pal, who animated *The War of the Worlds* (1953), and Ray Harryhausen, who worked on *Clash of the Titans* (1981).

Clash of the Titans (1981)

Today, almost all animation is computer generated, but this is a completely different approach from other forms of animation. With CG animation, a virtual world is constructed with computers, and characters and objects are programmed to move within that world. The virtual world is then virtually lit in the same fashion as a real film set, and a virtual camera is positioned to capture the action like a real camera in the real world. The biggest distinction with CG animation is that the basic rules of physics do not apply. Objects don't reflect light, they are light. Objects can stop moving instantly, or they can fly off without motivation. Two objects can occupy the same space at the same time, and there is no gravity. Nothing is impossible in a virtual world. Unlike classic animation though, the ultimate output of computer animation is not an acetate cel, but a digital file that can be combined with other digital images to create the final film.

The technology that made radio possible paved the way for "talking pictures," so it's no surprise that movie sound effects engineers can trace their roots to radio as well. The first radio dramas went on the air in 1921, often borrowing scripts from stage productions, but they didn't always translate well, because the audience couldn't see the action. Soon radio producers learned to create sound effects that could fill in the gaps and create a "theatre of the mind." While some sounds were recorded on phonographs, the quality of those sounds was far from pristine, and the phonograph itself would "hiss" and "pop" destroying the illusion. So, most sound effects were created live during the show. Sounds like footsteps and slamming door effects were common but sometimes sound engineers had to get creative because the actual sound of things didn't come across on radio. For example, a watering can pouring on a hard surface might substitute for a light rain but frying bacon will sound more like a heavy rainstorm. In reality, fire makes very little sound other than the occasional "pop," but cellophane being crinkled in front of a microphone has been used so often that many people accept the convention that fire actually sounds like that. Even though audiences can see the action in film (unlike radio), in the early days the microphones were not sensitive enough to pick up the sound of objects or ambient noise.

So, just as in radio, sound effects engineers were hired to create effects in post-production. Initially this was called "direct to picture" sound but beginning in the 1960's it would be called "Foley" after the most noted sound effects engineer in Hollywood, Jack Donovan Foley.

Jack Donovan Foley

Chapter Twelve – Effects

Foley, like many others in the industry in the 1920s was a real jack-of-all-trades. He was an actor, stunt man, writer, director, prop man, and much more. After the success of Warner Brothers' use of sound in *The Jazz Singer* (1927), Universal Pictures was anxious to jump on the bandwagon. Their first major sound film was *Show Boat* (1929), and they asked Foley to create the necessary incidental sounds. Because of the primitive state of recording, Foley developed a style of "performing" all the sound effects in a single take using specialized props that he either gathered or made. Often, he would need other people to assist in his sound effects making performance, and ultimately these acolytes went on to become Foley artists themselves.

Foley is still done in much the same way today, but innovations in recording, particularly digital recording, allow for much greater flexibility. Now each sound, including dialogue, is put on a separate track so that recording engineers have maximum flexibility in adjusting the final product. Even though the technology now exists to record sound effects live, Foley is still used to ensure that flexibility. Sound can now be stretched or compressed or looped so that it can be played over and over again. The pitch and reverb can be adjusted, and it can be equalized to achieve the maximum effect. With the use of computers and surround sound, effects can be created that would have been beyond Foley's imagination.

229

Of course, the use of computers has so profoundly affected the field of visual effects that they can hardly be referred to as "special" effects anymore; they have become a routine part of filmmaking. The first major film to use a computer for a special effect was *Westworld* (1973). In that film, it was simply used to create a pixelated image to represent how a robot might view the world. From that point forward, computers became increasingly involved in creating film effects.

Westworld (1973)

The biggest challenge to incorporating computers in film was speed. In the earliest days of CGI (computer generated imagery) computers were not powerful enough to create the effects we see today. Rendering a furry creature, for example, was quite difficult because it meant creating a mathematical equation for each hair on the creature. In time however, animators (and programmers) developed shortcuts for things like that, and computers became more and more powerful.

The concept of CGI in the age of digital motion pictures is somewhat straight forward. Each "frame" of a movie is now simply an array of colored pixels and because any pixel can be virtually any color, ultimately any image can be created. The trick is to efficiently use software and programming tools to accomplish these effects.

Films are artificial constructs. The images and sounds in the cinema are all an illusion. The purpose of special effects is to make these illusions seem entirely credible, or to take ordinary things and make them seem incredible. Effects will be effective (and affective) if they work in accord with other filmmaking elements to create a believable narrative.

KEY POINTS:

- Film is an illusion and effects are a major part of creating that illusion.
- There are three types of effects used in film: special effects, visual effects, and sound effects, but those names have changed to mean different things over the years.
- The first special effect in film history is seen in Alfred Clark's *The Execution of Mary, Queen of Scots* (1895).
- The first use of the term "special effect" was in 1939 by the Academy of Motion Picture Arts and Sciences.
- The term "special effects" refers to either "optical effects" or "practical effects," both of which are done while filming.

- Practical effects are any physical or mechanical illusion done in front of the camera.
- Props or scenery that are constructed to create an illusion are referred to as "practicals."
- The creation of atmospheric and weather illusions, such as rain, wind, snow, or fog, are also practical effects.
- Pyrotechnics and gunfire would traditionally be considered practical effects, but much of that is computer generated today.
- Armorers, pyrotechnicians, and stunt performers need to be employed to create these effects.
- The use of blood in film was kept to a minimum during the Motion Picture Production Code era (roughly 1934 – 1968).
- There are many types of fake blood (sometimes referred to as Kensington Gore) created for a variety of practical purposes.
- Specialized makeup techniques, often using foam rubber and latex, are another type of practical effect.
- Sometimes mechanical effects supplemented makeup effects to create a more fantastic look.

- Puppetry is one of the oldest practical effects in film.

- Then animatronics began to replace puppetry with robots, even though they are often clunky and unreliable.

- Optical effects can be thought of as optical illusions for film.

- "Rear projection" or "process" shots, which are achieved by filming action in front of a projection, can be technically difficult to achieve.

- Because the camera lacks depth perception, it is easy to incorporate classic optical illusions like "forced perspective" to create an effect.

- By using a lens that can keep both distant objects and near objects in focus at the same time, the relative scale of an object can be altered.

- The use of scale models can be effective, but they usually need to be shot in slow motion to scale down the physics of the scene to smaller proportions.

- The Schüfftan process uses a partially mirrored sheet of glass at a 45o angle to simultaneously capture the reflection of a model as well as action performed behind the mirror.

- A glass shot is when a partially painted piece of glass is placed in front of the camera to extend the background.
- Visual effects are usually created with an optical printer after the principal shooting has been completed.
- A combination of painted glass (mattes), or filters placed in the optical printer and the compositing of two or more film clips can be used to create the effects.
- "Day for night" shooting is when night scenes are shot in full light, but through a combination of underexposure and colored lenses in the optical printer, it gives the appearance of being shot at night.
- A traveling matte shot is a complicated process using colored lenses to create a matte that changes for each frame of film.
- Animation another optical effect that is achieved by placing a series of drawings inked on clear cellulose acetate (cels) into an optical printer.
- Rotoscoping is a type of animation that is created when an animator draws the cels over top of live action footage.
- Stop-motion animation involves shooting a film one frame at a time, while moving objects (often clay models) slightly between each frame.

- Today, animation is computer generate by filming a movie in a virtual world.
- Computer generated virtual worlds are not constrained by the physics of the real world.
- Movie sound effects engineers can trace their roots to radio.
- "Foley" (once known as "direct to picture sound") is a method of using specialized props to re-create sound effects in post-production invented by Jack Foley.
- Foley is still done today, but it is aided by digital recordings and computers.
- The use of computers has become so routine in filmmaking, that they aren't referred to as "special" effects anymore.
- With digital motion pictures, nearly anything that can be conceived can be created.
- The biggest challenge with computer generated imagery is the time needed to create it.

ENDNOTES

[1] Houpt, Simon. "De Laurentiis Keeps the Films Rolling." The Globe and Mail, The Globe and Mail Inc., 17 Apr. 2018, www.theglobeandmail.com/arts/de-laurentiis-keeps-the-films-rolling/article4139804/.

[2] Brockes, Emma. "George Lucas: No, Star Wars Is Not Supposed to Be Funny." The Guardian, Guardian News and Media, 16 May 2002, www.theguardian.com/culture/2002/may/16/artsfeatures.starwars

[3] Lauzen, Martha M. "The Celluloid Ceiling: Behind-the-Scenes Employment of Women on the Top 100, 250, and 500 Films of 2018." 2018 Celluloid Ceiling Report, Center for the Study of Women in Television and Film, San Diego State University, 2019 https://womenintvfilm.sdsu.edu/wp-content/uploads/2019/01/2018_Celluloid_Ceiling_Report.pdf.

[4] Jenks, Julia. "2018 Theme Report." Motion Picture Association, Motion Picture Association, Inc., 2019, www.motionpictures.org/wp-content/uploads/2019/03/MPAA-THEME-Report 2018.pdf.

[5] Salt, Barry. "THE METRICS IN CINEMETRICS." Cinemetrics, Cinemetrics, 2011, www.cinemetrics.lv/metrics_in_cinemetrics.php.

[6]Darnton, Charles. "This City has Over 500 Moving Picture Shows. Do YOU Know WHY?" The Evening World Daily Magazine, 1/16/1909, pg. 9. Web. 2/1/2018.
https://chroniclingamerica.loc.gov/lccn/sn83030193/1909-01-16/ed-1/seq-9/

[7]Kopiez, Reinhard, Anna Wolf, Friedrich Platz, and Jan Mons. "Replacing the Orchestra? – The Discernibility of Sample Library and Live Orchestra Sounds." PLoS One, vol. 11, no. 7, 2016, Web. 2/1/2018.
https://www.ncbi.nlm.nih.gov/pmc/articles/PMC4934781/

[8]Nichols, Bill. Introduction to Documentary. Indiana University Press, 2010

[9]Rodinson, Penseur. "'Loving Vincent' - How the Ignorati Killed a Masterpiece in Oil..." *Medium*, Medium, 13 Mar. 2018,
https://medium.com/@Penseur/loving-vincent-how-the-ignorami-killed-a-masterpiece-in-oil-c533c80262d3.